IN PRAISE OF TOADSTOOLS

All the pictures in this book are life-size

Frontispiece - Amanita excelsa - overleaf
the beech leaves around the stately Toadstool were cleared away with care to show the
unexpected length of stalk, a feature of this Amanita, and the young ones nestling beneath.
It was always good to look under leaves or earth for the beauty of a buried base, coloured
mycelium, or infant toadstools hidden from the casual glance.

3

IN PRAISE OF TOADSTOOLS

by Suzanne Lucas
FLS PRMS FPSBA SWA HSF

Aleuria repanda

For my Mother

Lucas Art

IN PRAISE OF TOADSTOOLS

by Suzanne Lucas
FLS PRMS FPSBA SWA HSF

Published by Lucas Art, Manor Road,
Mere, Warminster, Wiltshire BA12 6HQ

First published in Great Britain 1992 by Lucas Art

Designed by Lucas Art and Printed by Surdaw Press
Station Road, Gillingham, Dorset SP8 4PR

Printed Offset Litho onto Sovereign Silk from
Howard Smith Papers Limited

Colour Separations by Colthouse Repro Limited, Bournemouth

Bound by Cedric Chivers Limited, Bristol

British Library Cataloguing in Publication Data
A catalogue record for this
book is available from
the British Library

ISBN 0-9520456-0-5

VOLUME ONE

Lucas Art

Introduction

by Dr. Roy Watling B.Sc., Ph.D., D.Sc., F.R.S.E., F.I.Biol.
Senior Principal Scientific Officer and Head of Mycology at The Royal Botanic Garden Edinburgh

Fungi are the "cinderella" of botany, having only a limited number of admirers, and surprisingly they have rarely been considered when developing ecological concepts. This is strange as fungi play such important roles in the world's vegetation, including the re-cycling of nutrients during the decomposition process, and the capture of often otherwise unavailable nutrients, incorporating them into plant tissue. The grandeur of our forests and the expansive features of the prairies and steppes in large part relied on fungi for their formation.

It has always amazed me that in general botanists have not been enthused by fungi; true they are what is called heterotrophic, meaning they do not obtain their nutrients from the sun, water and air with the mediation of chlorophyll, but in what other group can you find the bizarre and ridiculous, the most cryptic colouration in juxtaposition with ranges of exotic colours, coupled with a whole variety of life-styles, strategies and shapes.

The most familiar examples of fungi are of course the mushrooms, eagerly eaten as an addition to our diet, and the toadstools which are so conspicuous in our woodlands and pastures in autumn. Such mushrooms and toadstools are simply the reproductive structures (fruiting bodies) of the fungi concerned. They are made up of minute cylindrical cells called hyphae and produce myriads of microscopic spores by which the fungi are reproduced and dispersed. The vegetative phase of fungi is also made up of an extensive network of these cells which, when massed together, form mycelia. The latter grow often unseen through the soil, wood or other medium, be it living or dead, from which the fungus is able to derive its nourishment.

Those that attack living tissues are parasites and are generally microscopic species. Many cause untold damage to crops and trees and some attack animals - just think of the ring-worm fungus. On the whole fungi cause annually an astronomical loss in most food production world-wide.

There are many more fungi, however, which do not attack living hosts causing disease. The mycologist calls them saprophytes and they range from microscopic forms to many of our large, familiar toadstools. There are many thousands of different species but thankfully only a small handful that affects man directly by rotting house timbers and food in store.

There are also toadstools which, although they infect the roots of living trees, do not cause disease but appear to improve the growth of their host, particularly when on poor soils. Such fungus - root relationships are called mycorrhiza and many of the partnerships are highly specific, some toadstools being associated with certain types of tree only. Lichens are a parallel association between species of microscopic fungi and not trees, but algae, and are of course some of the earliest colonists after any disturbance.

All these relationships and species add to the incredible reticulate patterns we now know and much of this can be observed in one's garden, park or local woodland. Add this to the beneficial fungi used in baking, brewing and the pharmaceutical industry, among others, and one has the fascinating world of the fungi.

Man's interest in fungi stretches back into pre-history and probably arose from the poisonous, hallucinating or edible properties of some species. Scientific interest began in the 17th Century and until the end of the last century was chiefly concerned with their naming and classification. At first interest centred on the larger fungi, but improvements in the design of microscopes made it possible to see the structure of the microscopic forms such as the bread moulds and mildews.

The reasons for illustrating fungi are as diverse as the rationale for studying them critically. Some of the earliest pictures were painted for decoration, but subsequently illustrations were produced to record the facts which stimulated deep fascination for fungi in artists and scientists alike. Some illustrations are simply personal aids to identification whilst others were created to illustrate books which either communicated the results of research or enabled others to identify fungi for themselves. There has also been an increasing number of fungi depicted on postage stamps.

The tendency in recent years has been to produce photographs of fungi but, however good they may be, only an artist can bring these organisms to life and make them objects of beauty and a correct record to help in identification and the study of variation. We have herein just such illustrations.

Author's Note

The book you hold in your hand is an eighteen year old dream come true. Fulfilled dreams are an expensive joy and you will be happy to know that the actual production cost of each volume was sixty-five pounds so that you may feel you have value for your outlay.

During those eighteen years I have worked steadily to prove that toadstools are a magnificent part of the world's natural heritage. This is at last taking effect: more and more books, pictures and even television are taking account of these enchanting creatures which is to my great satisfaction and joy.

For me personally the book is a love story which has, as evidence, the utmost that I could do to represent with truth and deep affection the ones I love at their best and most beautiful. My hope is that it will delight those who hold them dear and persuade some, who don't, of their quiet loveliness and gentle charm.

The area of toadstool naming has been described as a minefield. Enquiring, and in my innocence believing that a definitive answer would be proffered, I found that minefield. From two experts came different answers, or in some cases none from anyone. Once when I provided the spores themselves the conclusion did not fit the case. So there are pictures covered by the general term species and several are mysteries yet to be solved, of which one small puzzle is in the book. With the names some may argue, others say they are wrong. I can claim only to have done my best.

As to the pictures they are placed with beauty, not kinship, in mind. They are set with companions who harmonize or contrast with their colours and forms to give most pleasure to the eye. In order not to interfere with this in any way the captions are on the opposite page, often with a small toadstool picture as well, and the number is in the right-hand corner of the same page.

The technique used in painting is one of transparent glazes. This is not quite as simple as it sounds because X-ray eyes are needed to penetrate the outside layers of colour to the first one of all, which can be quite surprising. The golden-burnt sienna Tricholoma ustale began with yellow, progressed in some parts to bright mauve and only then went on to stronger gold and browns. Another needed full glazes up to a deep purple-brown then to be covered, using a very delicate touch, with a layer of soft gold-green velvet.* This method, sometimes using up to ten glazes of differing shades, gives the toadstool not only the right surface texture, but also conveys the strength of its substance.

The subtlety of toadstool colours, in painting realized from a quite restricted palette by sensitive variation of quantities, is a problem in print. For the colour separator, the printers, the type-setters struggling with uneven caption lengths and myself it has been a long, complicated and sometimes wearying endeavour to reach the quality a dream should have. Perfection may not be of this world but we think we are as near as is possible to the best, given the shortcomings of machines. Against these we have set all the human skill of hand and eye that could be mustered and hope the result may find favour.

Over the years much faith of others in my work has carried me through, above all my mother's, for her belief in a good final outcome never faltered despite many set-backs and disappointments. I remember Dr. Philip Findlay too, with affection and gratitude for his constant support up to his untimely death, which was a great sorrow to all who knew and loved his gentle and admirable character. He was so anxious that a book of my toadstools should be published and I wish he were here to see it now.

Also I am grateful in memory to the Marquis of Bath and Mr. René Hoare, and to their families, for their courtesy in allowing me the freedom of their lands to go where I wished in my search.

I would like to thank Dr. Roy Watling for his kind encouragement at the very beginning of my toadstool years, help with identification and the introduction to the book; Dr. David Pegler for time out of his busy day spent also in identification; Margaret Hayward for her tireless care in cleaning pictures from many years ago and helpful consideration in the choice and placing of the pictures; finally Brian Nicholson for much expert advice and, with the staff of the Surdaw Press, for patient perseverance in achieving colour exactitude and a well-presented book.

All this help and good will have brought "In Praise of Toadstools" from imagination to reality. I trust that it will create love and the same good will towards the many wonderful beings whose portraits it contains.

* to appear in Vol. 2

This is no learned treatise on Fungi, rather a collection of the thoughts and experiences of an artist who came suddenly and with astonished delight to what was for her an unexplored world, bringing at the beginning no knowledge, but an observant eye and immense appreciation. It is the story of many years spent searching for its enchanted inhabitants with the happy discoveries, unexpected encounters both beautiful and diverting, and the sheer enjoyment of stillness and peace in woods and fields.

For a long time I had, on occasion, found toadstools and thought them fascinating, but for some reason nothing more than a few pictures and miniatures on ivory came of it. Then one day in July 1974 a toadstool, pure amethyst from head to toe, appeared in my garden, was painted, and mushroom mania set in for good. Full of wonder at the perfection of our intriguing companions on earth, I wished above all things to show the beauty I had seen through my painting, for they are indeed a Third Kingdom in a wonderful creation. Is there anything nearer perfection than the pink gills of a young wild mushroom under a cream head, or the ethereal blue of a dawn-fresh Lepista nuda, the wood blewit? Not content with that, there are unsuspected layers of different colours as in Boletus regius, imperial purple splendour of head until a squirrel comes along and, nibbling a little, reveals layers of carmine and canary yellow beneath. Moreover the lovely gold stalk turns in four minutes to peacock blue and love-bird green where there was the pressure of handling. This surprising event lasts for forty minutes before returning to normal. Truly this is worthy of wonder and the protection they are trying to achieve for this paragon.

They needed an apologist to crusade in their favour. There are rare toadstools such as this, or even the commoner beauties, which are losing their habitats just as are the plants and animals. But they suffer from being so much unloved that they can become endangered and never would the general public care. At the last showing of my pictures a Czechoslovakian lady, who has lived in England since the war, told me of a wonderful stretch of woodland where hundreds of Boletus edulis grew, that kingly toadstool of marvellous flavour known in her country as The Gentleman. The bull-dozers and excavators have moved in: the wonderland of this most handsome creature is gone for ever in the name of yet another development.

Not until we begin to discover what they have meant and achieved in the ecological balance of our world shall we give them their due protection and value them for their usefulness and intrinsic beauty. True, there are those which are harmful: so there are plants and humans. Surely these inhabitants of a Third Kingdom have their place and we cannot tell what their absence might mean in damage and loss. There is a possibility that acid rain destroys these sensitive lives and trees die from the absence of their symbiotic companions, who keep them in good health, not from the rain itself.

Toadstools are such personal acquaintance. Flowers are appealing, they speak to the heart, they are variously exquisite in their perfection and universally loved, their validity is traditional and accepted millennia ago. Plants need no advocate. For toadstools it is otherwise. Perhaps dislike comes from their uncanny quality and their unpredictable comings and goings, but also has roots in an atavistic fear dating from far back in history when they, their lives and uses were reserved for the priesthood and to the people were taboo. Those with hallucinogenic properties, some as powerful as LSD, were employed by priests of ancient cults in initiation or other rites and five kinds are still in use in Mexico, some for group religious experience. One gives a sense of floating as proved by my mother in Paris when, attending the Opera after eating mushrooms at dinner, among which there was clearly an extraneous toadstool, she found herself continually floating upwards to the very splendid chandelier where she hovered, observing the whole auditorium and stage from above. These strange attributes and the sense of their personalities must explain why, in some countries, they were held to be magical at the least and at the most sacred in their own right, elevated to the ranks of the Gods, to be worshipped with due reverence.

On the continent the element of food has persisted, here the tradition of poison to fear and hate. I recollect seeing, as I drove past, a man walking along the verge crowded with bewitching Coprinus comatus, whacking each and every one down with his stick and treading on them for good measure. At least he could have made a delicious meal of them, had he known.

Continentally, where people seem long to have freed themselves from old influences and take a more pragmatic view, recognising the excellent culinary virtues of many fungi, difficulties with identification are few: most children in the country grow up knowing their toadstools by instinct or a pharmacist is always the expert at hand. In Germany all, whether edible or not, are so well-liked that each has a German name such as the Veiled Lady, the Shell-shaped little Dwarf Foot, a whole family of knights - the red, the green and the yellow, like the old song, and sounding quite mediaeval. The idea that toadstools are good to look for and eat is spreading due to the influence of european chefs, so it cannot be too strongly stressed that no toadstool should be cooked without absolute knowledge of its edible identity remembering that all old folk rules, such as silver spoons turning black, do not apply. Very few are deadly but some are extremely uncomfortable, against which many are excellent and most nourishing food. One mistake, though, is enough and the poisonous ones do not forgive for often the symptoms of poison are delayed until it is too late for treatment. An extraordinary one, Cortinarius orellanus, sometimes takes nine to fifteen days to manifest its presence but has been known to kill seven months after being eaten, which makes one wonder who the patient researcher was who managed to trace the death back to its cause.

This does not mean that the poison jumps at you: you have to eat a small piece first, but it does no harm to wash one's hands after touching unknown toadstools for complete safety. Which said, the poisonous quality of some in no way diminishes their loveliness for all of these are impressively beautiful. This fact has saved me from experimental cookery as it would seem like murder when they are in their pristine youth, then by the time their portraits are done they are inedible, whatever their kind may be.

Some shudder at the poison. How many of them remember the immense debt we owe to penicillin and the whole subsequent range of antibiotics, all inhabiting the same world, which have opened for multitudes the way to health and life. Moreover without the penicillins there would be none of the most succulent cheeses and without the other family of fungi, the yeasts, there would be no wine or beer or bread. Nor is this the end of the as yet uncalculated good done by the Third Kingdom in favour of animals of the First and green things of the Second as many sympathies, symbiotic relationships, exist between fungi and trees or plants. They are often of as great benefit to their neighbours in fields and woods as they can be to us, living in harmony each kind with its chosen companion and rendering mutual help to health and growth. Orchids, indeed, need a fungus in their earth and will not flourish unless it is there. Woodlands depend for their well-being on the underground mycelium of this remarkable creation whose beauty we can enjoy when the gorgeous fruiting growths appear.

Then why do people not recoil at the mention of a deadly plant? They think only of its charm and where it might look well in the border, to be fed and cherished. Yet the proud gardener hates the sight of a toadstool on his silken lawn, however innocent, never pausing to consider how lovable the small communities look - golden-brown, gold and scarlet, silver-grey, all against the bright green grass and in the most appealing shapes and sizes. Even some mycologists can be the same. Interested in construction, spores and identification, habitat and growth, they do not consider the sheer beauty of their subject. I said to one - isn't it wonderful? He looked a little surprised and supposed it was. Another who came annually to the Royal Horticultural Society Show to see my newest finds accused me roundly of beautifying my models. I replied that in many books the toadstool is painted half-dead with the pristine colours gone and who, after all, paints a fading rose? So here they are in this book, gathered and painted as they first glimpsed their world, from infants to adults, in their fresh glory of new growth.

For an artist discovering this uncharted realm, still ignorant of much but enamoured of the subject and full of enthusiasm, there were the twin pitfalls of pedantry about newly acquired knowledge and sentimentality, both tiresome to those who know All About Toadstools. I may be saved from the first by much continuing ignorance but the second is certain. Arriving in what to me is an enchanted and enchanting kingdom was such an unaccustomed joy that I must hope to find forgiveness for being fervent about a continuing devotion. The magic appearance of these small beings where the night before, or even hours before, was only bare wood or earth, gives a sense of treasure-trove; to set out on a search without any idea of what one may find rouses a feeling of adventure with, on each sortie, moments of happy surprise as, suddenly, there they are, unexpected and unknown new beauty. Sometimes it may be the glad recognition of an old friend. But then I feel guilty and

almost ashamed of my greedy hands when I collect such perfection, trying to be very gentle, for not only are many of them of great fragility but also they make a different impact from plants, asking to be treated with even more care and respect, and I find myself handling them as if I expected them to jump from my grasp back to freedom. This impression is hard to explain but a few others to whom I have spoken feel the same thing. Also one said that to have pictures of them in a room is companionable, another that she felt she had someone in the house and certainly, when I open the studio door in the morning where toadstools are waiting, unmistakable presences are there creating an atmosphere of their own.

This can happen with plants but they are more withdrawn in their aura and less close to us in their essence. With some of the toadstools which last longer I lived for days and this creates a wholly different awareness from collecting for dissection and scientific study. One learns much from watching them live and develop, while their presence imprints itself slowly on the mind in all its loveliness of line and form, then setting them outside after painting work is ended where they can still be seen each day. The large Psalliota sylvatica of the picture was too splendid to throw away, so I put it in a pot beside the studio door where it could not only be looked at by me, but also perched upon by my tame robin who found it most convenient as a landing stage for his visits to me while I was painting. The next spring he was, indeed, to bring first his wife, the gentlest robin I ever met, and later the whole resulting family for the always ready treat of nuts carefully broken into pieces.

The habitat can be of much interest with the quite unsuspected life around a model whose home, as well, has to be taken to the studio. There was the hollow log from the garden where grew Collybia velutipes, with flame-gold caps and sepia velvet-stockinged feet, which proved to be much appreciated for dinner by slugs. When I went to the studio one night to make sure that something which should have been turned off was not on, there they were, come from inside the branch, each slug enjoying its toadstool. My interest was aroused by the elegant and personal markings on these animals, some most beautiful and, as my picture of Velvet Feet was almost finished, I left them to their supper. Next night, deciding to see how they were getting on, I discovered them precisely as before; each slug, identifiable by its markings, was feasting on its own toadstool, not then or later interfering with anyone else's meal.

After that I went up often at the same time to see what was about, if some piece of wood or stone was in use. Peltigera canina spent a while with me on a large stone brought from the rockery, on which all manner of very small animals walked at night. Among them were minute snails with shells such as those which, with others, formed the chalk under the Downs, their tiny horns searching for a way over the mountain; insects like mobile forget-me-not seeds, tiny moths and the smallest possible spiders all going about their nightly business. Peltigera canina is of a most elegant appearance, frills of olive and blue-green lined with white beneath, from which long snowy needles point downwards, and bearing burnt sienna-coloured fruits. This is a relationship between a fungus and an alga (the sea-weed family) the first providing the fruiting bodies with spores and the mycelium, the second the greenery which can itself spread and an infusion of this was once considered a cure for the dreaded hydrophobia.

Observation led also to the discovery that particular creatures live with their own toadstools. A delicious group of specially opulent rosy Mycena haematopus brought with it the most diaphanous of flies, not unlike a miniature may-fly, all white but for a faint mother-of-pearl iridescence on its wings. This little insect did not leave its home either on the drive to the studio or during the time I painted, then travelled with the toadstools as I took them home to the woods. What did leave was the colour of the Mycena, gone by the next evening.

So it is with most of the fresh young colours, making for a constant race to catch the beauty before it flies. An amethystine blue of early morning will be ivory beige by ten o'clock, a deep purple rich enough for a king's mantle turn brown, or a toadstool collapse. One exquisite creature haunts me yet and I regret bitterly the afternoon I promised myself to fetch her the next morning. It proved to be full of intruding cares and when I went back she was gone nor has appeared since. There is a stubborn empty place where stood a perfect little umbrella, four inches across, rose and cream with dark brown velvet flecks and an edging of lace. I mourn, too, the jade-gilled ivory beauty on an elder log in the garden and the glowing brown thimbles, balanced on tall stalks, which grew during torrents of rain in a grass clearing, both lost to dutiful cares and not seen again. I did try to find the thimbles once more but was hampered by having discovered them on the only day that I lost myself in the woods, after wandering on my search whichever way instinct pointed for an hour or two. At least it was still daylight and, by keeping what seemed the lighter clouds in the same place, I calculated that I must reach a path or road in time. This I did, but even going back to that point I could not find the way to the toadstools which, of course, had collapsed while I was pre-occupied and afterwards painted others which deluded me into thinking them more fragile. Whenever it poured I looked for them but it was of no avail.

For two years the garden study kept me well occupied before I went further afield. By daily search one learns much of the lives and customs of these intriguing people and also discovers the entrancing and unconsidered small inhabitants. Some reappear in the same place whereas others have gone after one, or maybe two, appearances. Perhaps there are annuals, biennials and perennials; possibly it is a matter of differing lengths of the time between fruitings. But it does seem that those on more ephemeral homes, such as families of minute toadstools a tenth of an inch high which grew *only* in half filbert nutshells *two* years old, must be annuals reliant on the supply of the required food. Poppy seeds can wait a hundred years for open ground, surely spores are quite as patient. Above the roots of a dead apple tree left to tempt visitors Coprinus micaceus came up overnight in troops, their young heads golden-chestnut before they opened out to light brown parasols lined with sepia. The roots then supplied them with their requirements for some years.

For good measure the trunk of the same tree offered the magnificent sight of tier upon tier, three feet high, of cream brackets which were innocent in their life as they never moved to a live tree.

Some increase as did the wonderful Psalliota sylvatica. Its six-inch cap, speckled brown and cream with fine grey featherings and lined with shell-pink gills, came up under a camellia bush and returned each autumn for three years in undiminished splendour. Then suddenly the next year there was a positive planting of them as over fifty stood in noble array. I believe they are edible but I would not have dreamed of breaking a single member of that magical family. One waits for these perennials with the same expectancy as for the flowers whose garden they share and make lovely when autumn comes.

People have enquired, after seeing so many pictures of toadstools from my garden, how it comes to engender such variety to which I reply - sheer neglect. This is the first and perhaps the only rule for success, apart from a little clearing of ground for those who do not care to be jostled. Don't disturb, don't tidy, never burn a branch you can leave nor cut down an old tree. This was a productive rather than a vicious circle: because of my painting no time to clear rubbish, happy toadstools then finding welcoming homes on it and coming up ready to be painted. During that time of garden concentration it produced more than I could use, over two hundred to my knowledge and certainly more which eluded me. Never did it disappoint me on my daily search before I extended my hunting grounds to woods, marshes and fields.

A particularly rich source of treasures was the pile of old branches in the wild patch (not that most of the garden wasn't wild by then) which lay undisturbed for years. There all sorts of toadstools and cup fungi grew, from the tall Psathyrella conopilea with its sooty-dark bells at the edge in grass, to tiny fragile mycenas glowing like fire-opals on a branch covered with emerald moss. There, too, Coprinus lagopus appeared and taxed me sorely. It increased from a small soul enveloped in a velvety white coat to its full silver-grey stature of five inches between morning and afternoon, not keeping still ten minutes together. This was emulated by another member of the family (yet un-named) found nearby, a tiny white dot on the open end of a half-burnt wild parsnip stalk lying among old bonfire remains. I collected a spadeful of ash, sticks and leaves without disturbing the dot, put it in a flower-pot, watered it and waited on events. We raced each other. I painted it at hourly intervals and at seven changed to go out to dinner, after recording one more size. Home at midnight for two more sizes then and at 2 a.m. and, after a nap, at 4 and 6 a.m. At 10 o'clock the pearl-grey parasol, about three quarters of an inch across, was perfect for its final portrait. It grew again a fortnight later but how was I to know? One thing it proved - it was specific to open-ended half-burnt wild parsnip stalks.

A minute speckled cushion behaved in the same way, except that there were several at different times but one never knew *when*. It started off, after days of just sitting there, at express speed, turning into an apricot-coloured creation of delectable shape and then curling up into nothing before lunch. It defeated me finally by making a lightning appearance when business called me to London. The precious log where it lived was put by carefully for the next autumn but in vain.

Then came the year of drought and sensible toadstools remained buried in earth or wood so that it became also the year of the sphagnum bog study. Due to springs it was still damp and toadstools came up in their dozens, a whole new collection belonging there alone. Many are absolutely specific in their choice of ground or tree, kind of plant or dead wood such as those who will not consider anything but nettle stalks or fallen holly leaves. For some, moreover, the wood must be of an exact age and when they have lived out their time upon it, exhausting their own particular food, they hand it on to the next inhabitants who will find their needs, until the procession breaks down the log and returns it to the earth, neatly recycled.

By watching those which do return there are other discoveries such as the extraordinary variability of Coprinus romagnesianus of which there are two portraits in the book. I found the toadstool at the base of an aged oak post and two years running the brown caps appeared in all their charm of colour and pose; but what was my surprise the third year to see larger soft grey caps, as delightful in grace of form, but completely different. Yet both came from the same mycelium and showed the characteristics by which both Dr. Watling and Dr. Pegler identified them. It is possible that they are very sensitive to variable conditions and if we studied toadstools well they might tell us what to expect and help us to avoid some of the earth's disasters.

Armillaria mellea varies much from tree to tree, pale pink or gold, sometimes nearly brown, it always has a decoration of soft dark scales on its cap and a collar round a stalk which is mostly patterned in pink, red and brown or even purple at the base. One on an apple stump had pale gold caps like slender fluted glasses, with chequered bands on the stem from deep rose at the top to violet purple below.

This Armillaria has an unhappy reputation for slaying trees though I have seen so many of them year after year by the same trees which go on looking fighting fit. It appears now that there are varieties which do kill them, also those which benefit by living only on wood already dead. However that may be from the artist's point of view this is a splendid family. A rare sight, when I drove down an unaccustomed road one day, was the acacia variation on the stump of what must have been an outstanding and lovely tree, now home to a great concourse of toadstools whose caps, inches across, were white shading through to umber and ebony at the centres. They were some of the most impressive and original in colour and size I had seen and, as there was a meeting to attend, I was determined to come back next day. When I arrived toadstool phobia had been there first and the lovely things, of such rarity as never to be found again, had been torn down and trampled into muddy pieces on the road. Such wanton destruction of quiet beauty was really heart-breaking.

Another gorgeous exhibition was given by Armillaria polymyces, majestic shapes growing rank upon ever higher rank on an enormous sweet-chestnut stump. There were countless pure gold caps, umbrella-like at first, then turning upwards in fantastic wavy-edged hats of infinite imagination. The gills were light coral and the stems shaded down to a muted violet. I looked long, but not long enough, for two days later they were gone and I was left with one inadequate picture. The fruitful stump, handsome and sculptural in its own right, was removed as being unsightly.

It is hard to understand that many people think of toadstools, if they think of them at all, with a revulsion they cannot even explain; but certainly they miss the sight of some of the most exquisite symmetry in creation, reminiscent of sea animals such as the serenely graceful sea lilies which are living yet static. Because their way of existence and nourishment is not as the plants, but more as ourselves, living on organic food and breathing oxygen to sustain them, they have been classed in one quarter as animals. Protista, perhaps, the kingdom of organized beings neither animals nor plants.

This is debatable but may not be so far-fetched as it seems for the myxomycetes, or slime fungi, begin as creatures like infinitesimal tadpoles which have tails (scientifically flagella) and swim in water after "hatching" from spores. They land and conglomerate to form a fungus which can and does propel itself with a perfect sense of direction dictated by the cells at the forward end. One professor mentions his astonishment when he saw one of these climbing over the window-sill into his study. How can one think of it other than as an animal? Yet then it settles and produces spores, like any self-respecting fungus, which must find water to begin the cycle again. Toadstools are beings indefinable except as themselves but have seeming affinities with, and references to, so much varied life. Their success is indisputable. They have remained the same for millions of years and their origins are lost in time. However this may be their delicate construction is miraculous. To hold a toadstool upside down in your hand is to marvel that anything so fine as each gill and the setting of them all in an infinite circle can exist: purest white, pearl grey, shell-pink, rose, rich tobacco, cream, gold, peach, mahogany, mouse-brown, amethyst, mushroom and purple, almost all with tiny sparkling points where the light catches them. The caps and stalks extend the countless colours and shapes, yet the palette used is not wide. I have learned from toadstools the numberless shades realizable by mixing varying quantities of paint from the basis of so few colours and been astonished. They are too beautiful in colour and proportions, admirable in detail and impeccable in form, ever to be treated with anything but kindest care. Also it is a constant cause for wonder that the simple vertical and horizontal lines can allow of such infinite variation. Given that there are several thousand toadstool-shaped fungi a painting must be of absolute precision to achieve an exact likeness. Moreover there is never a mean-looking curve or corner, every line is unimpeachable and artistic interpretation has no place here. We wonder at the diversity of the human face, but there nature has many features to play with in presenting a unique and recognizable character. In toadstools there are only these two essential lines yet each small creature is a character in its own right, an individual which must be painted to make it stand alone among all its companions, even of the same kind. Therefore the important rule is to treat the toadstool as a small person whose portrait it is, a unique individual different from all others, even if they come up in their hundreds or thousands.

I remember going to the woods one day after much rain to find a perfect fairyland before me. The silent trees stood above a forest floor of red-brown spruce needles which was alive with numberless ethereal crowds of miniature pleated silver-grey bells balanced on slender stems only three or four inches high. Of all ages, they were scattered singly or in groups as far as the eye could see and it was hardly possible to walk without crushing some of that captivating and transient company. Yet no two would be exactly alike.

The happy search went on through cloudless days and also through floods, mist and pouring rain. On such a day I went to the marsh to find it soaking wet, even the warm air was mist-laden and the trees around spirit-like in the opalescent atmosphere. There I saw the most ephemeral creation I have ever found, of a delicacy beyond belief, which came and went within an hour or two. Growing on the bright green sphagnum moss it lay like large snowflakes and had exactly the same crystaline sparkle and purity. So far nobody can tell me what it was except for suggestions that I was deluded and it *was* snow; unlikely, it being one of the warmest, calm days we had that September. Further, it was attached to the moss anyway, so the mystery remains until some wise mycologist sends me a long Latin name which I hope will be as beautiful.

It was a magic day with apparitions never found again, creatures of water that disappeared or shrivelled into nothing as they dried. A strange animal was abroad in my garden looking like an extra thick horse-hair, seemingly with neither head nor tail, about twelve inches of it gently waving about but not going anywhere in particular. It too faded away with the heavy mists.

One loveliness did survive long enough to paint, for the same day the whole of the sphagnum bog burst into a host of pale rose-coral Paxillus involutus, a light brown person in ordinary times. Everywhere one looked there they were, beautifully shaped and curved, shining against the brilliant green of the moss round the silver-white trunks of birch trees. There are a few such happy days, remembered for ever, of unspoilt magic in perfect serenity and peace.

This beautiful little area, with the graceful silver birches turning to pure gold in autumn, so rich in toadstools and the source of much that was beautiful and rare, is itself only a memory now. On an unhappy day I went there for my usual quiet hour of discovery, as for years past, to stand suddenly in deep shock and disbelief. The birches were gone, their branches piled feet deep across the little marsh, their silver trunks sent to the brush factory. I sat down on the bank and wept. It was little consolation to be told that, had the owner known, the trees would have been spared. Another very special habitat, overflowing with interest and seemingly too small for harm, had gone for a few pounds just because nobody knew of its natural value. So one must never say to-morrow to a toadstool - it must always be to-day if at all possible, for that is the only certainty. Even then they don't always do what is expected. I hover thoughtfully over a collection wondering which will survive the longest, choose what looks least durable, and paint as if possessed. Those are the ones which smile happily three days later whereas the others, unchosen, will have passed on their silent way. But never must a painting be hurried: it is a matter of time and yet more time, never speed.

Toadstools are clearly not models hired by the hour. In no sense does one control them, they rule you: not aggressively or petulantly, nothing to rouse resentment but everything to claim devotion, not by demanding, but simply by their fleeting exquisite being. It is the same as loving birds or any other wild thing. One expects nothing more than the privilege of caring which will bring with it the joy of free companionship. Therefore this is the most satisfactory expression of love because, asking nothing, it is never disappointed or disillusioned.

All this should be taken calmly, a day's work done and put by, but that is impossible: every hour must be filled to avoid at least some of the sense of irrevocable loss when a real beauty is gone, in all likelihood never to return. Indeed the dear little souls keep one at it for they come up in bewildering variety and never wait longer than their short allotted time.

Added to this is the knowledge that life is not long enough to paint more than a fraction of the thousands there are, which makes for a double sense of urgency leading to work at a high level of awareness and at full stretch. This is excellent for pictures, less so for nerves, and in the height of the toadstool rush from July to November tension mounts and much sleep goes by the board, as does all else not concerned with the work in hand. Weeds grow in the garden, the house lies quietly under a cloak of dust, an egg is boiled and eaten rather grudgingly, the painting goes on.

Fortunately it is possible to paint a drawing, made accurately in all details, with the help of another member of the family, provided there are notes on colours. Thus it is well to bring home all stages from infant to adult, draw without respite and then judge, from what is happening before one's eyes, where to start. With luck they will all look well though the small ones need immediate attention before they overtake the grown-ups. It is a matter of fine judgement but with experience one can finish a nice family group. I remember waiting a long time to paint Coprinus comatus and had farming friends on dawn-watch at an inhospitable patch of rough grass such as they like. At five-thirty one morning the phone rang - they are up, announced my friends. In ten minutes I was away with a selection of baskets and bowls and gathered every age from the very tiniest only just visible. For this unbelievably lovely toadstool, its cream cap fringed with delicate flounces all the way down the slender cone-shaped head, is a very fast mover which grows as you watch it. It also sheds spores, black and in millions, followed soon by the gentle drip of an unctuous black fluid which makes excellent ketchup but is less desirable in a paint-box or on a picture, both needing protection. So one works, puts the aging model in a basin and takes another which has meanwhile grown to the right size. Meals are ignored, the table and studio over a six-foot circle disappear under finest black powder and painting continues with a scarf over mouth and nose as the spores make one feel rather odd. Another toadstool, Amanita excelsa, caused me to mask up for those spores made me feel sick, perhaps because the Amanita is poisonous, but so beautiful that it is all well worth-while.

The same friends took up their telephone to announce the exciting presence of Lycoperdon giganteum, an enormous puff-ball which I settled on a comfortable cushion for the return journey. Luckily it was not, as it has been known to achieve, the size of a sheep, but merely a lamb. It was still good enough when painted to allow me to try a slice for supper after peeling off a skin like finest chamois leather. Cooked in butter it is excellent but needs plenty of mashed potato to mitigate the richness of its taste. Perhaps a younger one would have been less forceful.

Devotion is the order of the day and particularly so when I painted another memorable visitor, the gem with the descriptive name Phallus impudicus which I prefer to Stinkhorn as nothing so beautiful should be so insulted, even if it is the truth. It is simple to find by following one's nose. I took it home in the young innocent stage, a quite innocuous, ivory, egg-shaped object which I painted before putting it in a plant-pot in the garage while waiting for further developments. It sat for a day or two considering, then suddenly the ivory sheath split to show a cap of exquisite green. That day I painted two further stages with much self-congratulation at finding the smell endurable. Little did I know. The next morning I needed a mask to get into the garage where the full-grown toadstool, in all its elegance and looking as if carved out of green and white jade set in an ivory and gold base, gave off the most incredible smell it has been my misfortune to meet. All, of course, for the benefit of flies who are attracted to the sweet and highly perfumed syrup on the cap and pick up the spores on their small feet for distribution abroad. Out in the woods the odour was unattractive, imprisoned it was indescribable. Work for two days was not amusing. It was cold and there was a high wind blowing: with door and both large windows opposite wide open I huddled, shivering in layers of winter coats, with mittened hands and face wrapped in scented scarves and still the smell was awful. My neighbours enquired what on earth I had in there, went back into their house and shut every window. It made a lovely picture and when it was finished I put the toadstool in the car and, with much self-sacrifice, drove it home to the spruce woods.

Painting toadstools is hard and intensive work, but the search for them is sheer joy and enchantment with a sense of expectancy, many times well rewarded by happy encounters and unawaited events. The woods around are a source of never-ending satisfaction. To set off in the sweetness of early morning without any idea of what may be found, or happen and be seen in the finding, is a constant pleasure. It is then that the new-born colours are most likely and one's steps are accompanied by the dawn chorus, the cries of the waking pheasants and often the bark of a fox or a vixen's eerie scream. Between the trees a stag lifts his head, crowned with brand new antlers, to test the wind. Pheasants I saw often, but one day I heard a curious thudding like distant galloping hoof-beats and, standing motionless, I could hardly believe my eyes when two foxes appeared along the path and raced by, four feet from me. It seemed impossible that such soft feet could resound like that from so far away. Many minutes passed before I moved on: I was lost in memory for they had been a most lovely sight, burnished golden-red against the fallen beech-leaves, racing on dark velvet feet with their tails streaming out behind them.

In looking for toadstools the best results cannot be expected if you hurry and so the search is the most restful and quiet pursuit imaginable. You don't find the precious ones by marching briskly over hill and dale; you take two or three paces, stop, meditate on your surroundings with a careful look about you, then venture a couple more and in this way find treasures as well as reaping the bonus which is a gift in the hands of stillness. The birds and animals take no fright at the slow inconsequential movements so like their own. There is a marsh not far away where once I found a small but very rare fungus whose rarity I discovered when it was long dead and had joined the sad list of the lost. At evening time, after providing some new treasure which it never fails to offer, it is a place of peace and delight. The birch trees are still, a newt lies in clear green moss, his brilliant orange tummy showing as he turns over lazily; a mouse goes past in no hurry; a squirrel, unbearably inquisitive about this new "tree" as I stand in silence, approaches in tentative scurries right to my feet. I move my eyes which, being unnatural in a tree, alerts the squirrel who changes his mind about climbing and is off. Hundreds of baby frogs and infant toads, tadpoles startled to find themselves presented with legs and all trying them out for the first time, watch jewel-eyed, moving at the last moment when a foot treads too near them. There are such happy numbers sitting alert or leaping about delightedly, that one steps with infinite care. The deer come down to the stream to drink and regard me gently, perhaps wondering what manner of creature I might be, and pheasants make their sharp evening calls as they go to roost.

Reluctantly I leave and go on to the beech woods. In the windless quietude after sunset one can hear the talk of the trees, tiny cracklings and murmurs as they settle down for the coming night. Astonishingly, long after grass and moss have lost their form toadstools, even the brown ones, still stand clear to be seen. As if the dusk could not enclose them they glimmer with a light of their own, holding the day in their hearts. I have found some of the most enthralling ones on the verge of darkness, once searching on as a honey-coloured full moon rose behind two tall beech trees, floating between their silver trunks in a sky of sunset-reflecting rose and blue.

For the seeker after toadstools the ways to discovery are many and various: garden observation, sorties in the car, telephone calls and sheer by-the-road good luck as well as rare guests whom I had never hoped to see but who come visiting. There are heart-warming help and kindness along the way as well as hazards in variety.

In the sphagnum bog on a day of torrential rain I was trying to reach a brilliant golden temptress on an island when I trod unwarily and sank deep, wondering if and when I might stop or was this the end? Drowned in pursuit of a toadstool. Fortunately it was not a bottomless pit and with much squelching I managed to extricate my bedraggled self, not even losing my Wellingtons in which there was an interesting collection of flora and fauna.

One evening when my strange propensities were yet unknown, the gamekeeper at Stourhead came past at dusk on his round to catch pheasant poachers of which he assumed I was one. It was a difficult moment and for a while I was under arrest waiting for the police, but set about explaining myself. Even to me it did not sound convincing, but was so far-fetched in Mr. Keeble's eyes that he believed me and was comforted to find that I knew nothing of the pernicious habit of lifting sleeping pheasants from their branches at night.

Another evening when I was collecting later than usual, my car was unrecognised in the dark and a search was made with much halloo-ing to find the thief who was after a tasty meal of deer or pheasant. Wide-eyed surprise greeted me as I walked forward making reassuring noises from behind a very large bowl of the enormous flower-like Paxillus I had gone back to collect. What was I going to do with that lot? Eat them? Instead of pheasant and deer I replied and all was well. Which reminds me, this toadstool is still quoted in some books as edible but recently it has been found to be detrimental over a period of time. It is best left to be beautiful where it grows, for the eye alone.

From then on, whenever we met, he asked after my discoveries and if he found me wrestling with an over-sized log sprouting delectable coral-rose shells or other fascinating growths he would brace himself and, with muscles cracking, load it into my long-suffering boot. Moreover he told me where he fed the pheasants so that I could wait silently and see them come for dinner, gorgeously dressed for the occasion. I owe him a debt of gratitude for his help.

Sometimes one chases the toadstools but sometimes also the light, for there is a remarkable phenomenon when, with a westering sun, the light intensifies and the magic begins. It happens in the countryside too, as mellow old brick houses respond with a warm glow, trees become luminescent and so do the toadstools on the table. They pick up the light in their myriad water-filled cells and shine back at you with an inner brilliance of their own. An orange cap will burn like living flame, a grey one gleam with an undertone of shell pink, a scarlet one sing with vivid tones. Then is the time to paint without pause endeavouring, however unsuccessfully, to catch something of this incandescent impression. There must be a quality in the texture of the cells of these ever-surprising creatures which reflects the light, after enhancing it with their own colour, and the afternoon draws out most beauty as it does in the landscape. There however, it is an effect of the slanting rays whereas the toadstools hold and increase the indirect glow.

Later afternoon is also a lovely time to go searching and often quite as rewarding for toadstools come up entirely when they have a mind. As the evening stillness envelops the woods, the sinking sun lights up the tree trunks and sometimes a golden shaft will pick out a large toadstool like a prima donna on a stage. The woodland floor shines and at larch-needle fall for two or three days this can be spectacular. The fresh needles are an indescribable colour of intense flame-rose, toadstools stand out so clearly that they call to one and birds sing their last and best before they sleep. Other provenances of fascinating subjects were brought to my notice by helpful people. One night, after a particularly hard day in London, I reached home at ten o'clock ready for bed. My mother telephoned "Darling, there are tomato-red toadstools on the lawn". Wearily I re-opened the garage, knowing full well that the colour would be short-lived, and drove to collect them by torchlight ready for a dawn start the next morning. I was grateful once more to my dictum - Never tomorrow - for they did not visit us again.

Another day a friend summoned me post-haste to collect the enchanting little Coprinus cothumatus decorating her cellar. It loves warm cellars and heated greenhouses and its apricot caps last radiantly but a few hours before turning brown, still most appealing but not the delicious golden-pink thimbles of its first delicate manifestation which I managed to catch just in time. It was a fruitful cellar for later on my friend said "I ordered a new load of logs and now there is something coming up on them". What would I have done without my faithful companion, the car? Responding at once to the call I found a most interesting version of Velvet Feet - Collybia velutipes - but this time without attendant slugs. Here in the cellar with reduced light it had grown in quantity, small and slender, still apricot and wearing velvet socks, but hardly enough for anyone's meal. Which is interesting: few of the small toadstools seem to be eaten.

Then there was a friend of mine who kept a horse in the back garden of her house in Bath from which animal she was able to make a nice pile of useful manure. Now some of the most beautiful toadstools find the richness of manure much to their taste. There came the familiar telephone summons and it was off to Bath where we decided to meet in the well-appointed lounge of a very nice hotel which served an excellent tea. My friend arrived bearing a plastic bucket filled with tall toadstools comfortably ensconced on a bed of their home ground which sat beside us, preciously guarded, while we enjoyed the tea. The waitress was much intrigued and most understanding when we explained.

On occasion toadstools spring into view by sheer good fortune as on a day when I was arrested by the sight of dozens of immense cream-gold Lepiotas, nine inches or more across, with shaggy brown scales in symmetrical circles on their caps and splendid strong mole-grey and pink stalks. They were visible from four hundred yards away, growing in the corner of a cow and bull inhabited field. The animals were in the distance and, trusting that the bull was more interested in the cows, I crept through a very workmanlike barbed wire fence (never wear the best clothes on such outings), collected a bowlful of these really gorgeous creatures and was surrounded, on reaching home, by marvelling neighbours who rushed for a camera. Lepiota rhacodes is edible and good if you have a very large frying pan and the heart to put such a lovely and noble creation into it.

Another time my mother and I were coming home at mid-night after a pleasant dinner. Suddenly I stood firmly on the brakes and came to an abrupt halt. As I reversed my mother, mildly surprised, saw the reason - a host of Lycoperdon perlatum, dramatically floodlit by the headlamps, much larger than they are supposed to be and so fresh that they seemed that instant grown out of a bed of beech-leaves. My mother supported them on her knees for the drive home thus giving me one of the toughest assignments ever. This Lycoperdon is a soft beige puffball, round-headed on a wide base and covered from head to toe with an intricate pattern of tiny points and dots, like seed pearls, from white to pale golden-brown. As long as they were in the studio they behaved in an exemplary fashion for which I was grateful as the spores, if breathed in, are poisonous. In due course they joined others in various pots and dishes which, with logs, trip up my visitors. It was fascinating, when the tops opened to release the spores, to see that on dry days nothing much happened but in wet weather, as each raindrop fell on one or other of them, a puff of golden-brown smoke shot into the air and one, believe it or not, blew an excellent smoke ring, encouraged by a particularly large drop.

My mother was a perfect companion as her enthusiasm and interest matched mine and one day, as we drove past the great beeches of Longleat, we saw a perfect group of Pleurotus ostreatus. The ones they now sell in shops can in no way compare with them for they were deep grey blue with pink gills, extremely desirable and just as high up on a beech trunk, so proving conclusively the usefulness of tools. A trowel is obvious, but a potato peeler is better for fine work, a chisel, a saw when faced with an impossible log and a hoe is perfect for such work as I had in hand. I did not have this useful implement, only a car-jack handle, and never have I had to leap so high to achieve the desired object. My mother watched enthralled but could not help as she was nursing a young bird which had been stunned by a car, we supposed. As I returned triumphant the bird, revived by warmth, took off out of the window so the Pleurotus was able to take its place under my mother's tender care.

It was an interesting subject which, excellent for our tables, is also an absolute passion with maggots. They were at work in no time and while I painted there was a steady small plopping sound as they fell, replete, and presumably ready to pupate. I felt they could do this elsewhere and every half-hour stopped to sweep them up gently and put them out of the window.

Toadstools on trees led to two other interesting occasions. One day my friend Sue Burton and I set off for a Private View half way across England with not a toadstool in mind. We were passing a row of majestic old oak trees when I startled her by turning right round with cries of *Look*. To quieten me she braked and backed, but was herself impressed at a good three feet of layers of cream, gold and pink rising up a trunk. We marked the place on the map and, our Private View done, called back and knocked on a nearby cottage door. The

farmer was surprised, then full of interest. Of course we could go into his field but mind the horses, the cows, the donkey, some geese and a goat - and it was muddy. No wonder with all that livestock in it. We asked if he had a hoe. Today a multiple plough will work many furrows at once: happily this was an old-fashioned farmer who led us to an ancient shed full of the tools of yesteryear. He opened the creaking door and invited me to make my choice, a museum worthy very long-handled hoe with which we set off, still in high-heeled shoes and cocktail dresses. The trek across the field can be left to the imagination as all the animals seemed to consider us fair game for their inquisitive noses and the mud was sticky. Arrived at the tree Sue took the hoe and with well-aimed strokes tried to dislodge the most magnificent Phaeolus sulphureus imaginable. She decided on caution, afraid to damage the quarry, and handed the hoe to me. That fungus loved its home and was extremely tough. I still persevered while Sue darted to and fro with outspread skirt to be sure of catching this splendid and precious thing. Successful at last we returned the hoe with many thanks and the good farmer said "Well I never" and took us off to see a whole lot of other toadstools whose names he wished to know.

The second incident involved the force of the law, for I am indebted to a charming West Country policeman for the completion of a picture which had been waiting three years. Two of us went to the Farnborough Air Show and, driving along the last stretch of lane, I saw on a tree in a birch wood the beautiful bracket fungi of the unfinished picture, in every required size. My companion suggested that we stop on the way back, an unrealistic idea as anyone who has been to the show at Farnborough will know. There we were, stuck in a miles-long stream of cars which would have lost a race with a snail. But there were the brackets and even a good clearing by the road so, to much indignant hooting, I turned out of the traffic and stopped. A tall policeman loomed up and told us that nobody, but nobody, was ever allowed to stop there - intense security, no-go zones and the like. Going into my explaining routine I told the bewildered young man what I wanted and all the whys and wherefores. Well, he said, be quick. The place was surrounded with barbed wire which he kindly held up for me, but when I got to the trees the fungi were too high to be reached even with the ever ready car-jack. I had not thought to bring a hoe as being unnecessary at an air display. I went back to my policeman and appealed to him. He muttered desperately "You will get me dismissed from the Force if the Inspector comes by" but did not let me down. He set aside his helmet and jumped repeatedly until we had a goodly set of brackets to take to the car where Jeremy was quite helpless with laughter. That courteous policeman then went the second mile by holding up the entire stream of traffic and slotting us in to go happily and very gratefully on our way.

So it goes on, collecting encounters with people of great interest, animals, plants and an increasing number of toadstools and other fungi. I have painted nearly four hundred of them, exhibiting the pictures at the Royal Horticultural Society shows every February since 1975, with thirteen Gold Medal awards for the work. Along came a truffle enthusiast one year when there was a painting of Tuber aestivum, a British representative of the edible ones. It appeared in my garden under a filbert, pushing half out of the ground to make sure that I found it. Once we had met I could find them by the strange perfume and also if I saw one of the bright burnt sienna flies, addicted to cow-pats, sitting on the ground I knew there was a truffle beneath - they loved them.

The enthusiast wanted to make a film featuring this truffle to show that the Italians and French were not the only ones to have them. The plan was to use a pig to do the traditional digging and I was to supply a likely beech wood. Autumn passed, I put the truffles into the fridge, winter slipped away and suddenly in early spring they announced they were coming. Only it wasn't truffle time, the ones in the fridge were not in their first youth and the wood was carpeted with bluebell leaves. I had to drive in haste to find a suitably autumn-looking wood and await events. They came in true television style with a convoy of large cars containing cameras, camera crews, much recording equipment, recording experts, a direction team of five, the owners of the pig, a few who had come along for the ride and in one of the car boots the pig itself - a large black sow who had slept peacefully all the way from Kent to Dorset. We went in procession to the wood, ate the loaves and butter and about four pounds of cheese I had brought, then unpacked and when everything was ready we woke the pig and the fun began. She'd had a wonderful sleep, was raring to go and furious to find herself in a strange land. She was on a very long rope which left her masses of scope. She charged and the target group scattered. We all scattered in turn, taking refuge with assorted equipment behind a bank. She charged time and again, oblivious of one human desperately hanging on to the other end of the rope, but no match for her at full tilt. She then decided, there being no more quarry in sight, to circle at the full length of the rope. At the other end the holder tried to get support from a tree. As the pig went round and round, squealing with indignation, it took some agility on his part not to be tightly bound to the tree. The pig went on regardless and I shall never forget the look of enraged bewilderment in her eyes when the rope gave out and she was snout up against trunk with nowhere to go. That calmed her down at last and when we unwound her, with some misgiving, she was quite docile and co-operated with me, cheek by jowl, in digging up the truffles I had planted and it was all nicely filmed. But the best part was never filmed, with the camera crew far too busy hiding behind trees or banks to film it.

On another occasion, to make a programme for the Aquarius series, the whole panoply of television descended on my studio. There were a generator van, huge spotlights, full recording equipment, macro-lenses and a crew of about ten to film my miniatures, the technique of painting them in progress (a special lens over my shoulder with a spotlight generating tropical heat), flower pictures and the toadstool study. After the studio we worked the garden, where I crawled through the grasses commentating on toadstool search and

discovery, and then repaired to the woods where the day before I had pin-pointed nice toadstools worthy to be film stars. It was a long and fascinating day brought to a close in late evening when the film ran out. The Aquarius series came, exactly then, to an abrupt end, so the work languishes in a forgotten corner.

Such colourful occasions were not everyday events. These continued to be looking, learning, enchantment and hard work, with the resulting contentment of a mind refreshed by community with the grace of natural things. Still the enticing thought of new wonders drew me on, sometimes through great trees with noble trunks and, rounding one, to be astonished by a magnificent splendour two feet across, red-brown velvet with a gold border, in super-imposed layers; or a pile of dried sticks turned over carefully might yield a rarity, a hollow branch a whole colony, or the marsh be lighted up by the clear yellow of Russula claroflava. What a family, with more amazing colours than any other: scarlet, crimson, purple, pink, blue, brown, olive, blue-green and tawny. The last I collected, among other toadstools, and on the way home was puzzled by a scent of violets in the car. Applying my nose to each inmate of the back seat in turn I discovered it to be the modest Russula fellea which then proved a most delightful model.

In spite of all that we know the scientific interest in toadstools is comparatively recent. They keep their allure and much of their mystery, neither the study nor the yearly addition of new kinds being anywhere near complete. Of the subjects in my pictures quite a few remain un-named and a doctor of mycological science told me that it was quite possible I had indeed found new sorts as, at the time he spoke, about a thousand a year were still being listed, though many of these would be moulds and microscopic fungi of which there were already over a hundred thousand.

The new surprise is that the whale must be considered a puny creature beside an Armillaria spread through fifteen hundred acres in America and which may be a thousand or more years old. A smaller family member inhabiting forty acres is estimated to weigh a hundred tons which, on a ratio basis, makes our giant weigh a possible three and three quarter thousand tons, a mighty life. This amazing living organism must have a most sophisticated central intelligence system, sensitive to its furthest part, for it closes down operations where food is unavailable, re-opening them when a supply arrives.

Moreover on a small scale we know that though toadstools were sometimes gods, they were also helpful servants as the two carried, probably for tinder, by Iceman in his pack over five thousand years ago.

Surely we must stand amazed at this kingdom, the properties and personalities of its subjects, their freedom and independence which gladden the heart. They are the exquisite wild things which come and go as they please. Our duty is to cherish and protect, admire and be grateful that we have been given such richness of beauty as a great natural treasure to enhance our lives.

Boletus edulis
a splendid example of the monarch of edible toadstools, magnificent in colour and form,
strength and firmness of growth, a truly grand creation appearing under beech trees in their
prime. It was three years before I found the perfect youngest one to complete the picture.

Lycoperdon umbrinum
was growing in grass with meadow plants, a
comfortable and charming shape in soft
mushroom brown with a fine decoration of
minute flecks.

Tubaria conspersa
many toadstools vary in a way bewildering to the artist, as this Tubaria with the
woolly feet I love, not new, just different.

Lactarius rufus
of a good size and gorgeous mahogany-red,
these grew under spruce looking most
harmonious against fallen needles on the
woodland floor.

Inocybe napipes
under spruce at the edge of a birch and
sphagnum moss fen, they had the enchanting
caps, typical of this family, to perfection.

Lepiota acutesquamosa
was a lesson in patience to paint and also
passionately sought after by snails, making it
difficult to find one with its shining white
perfection of gills intact. It came up four
years running under a crab-apple tree.

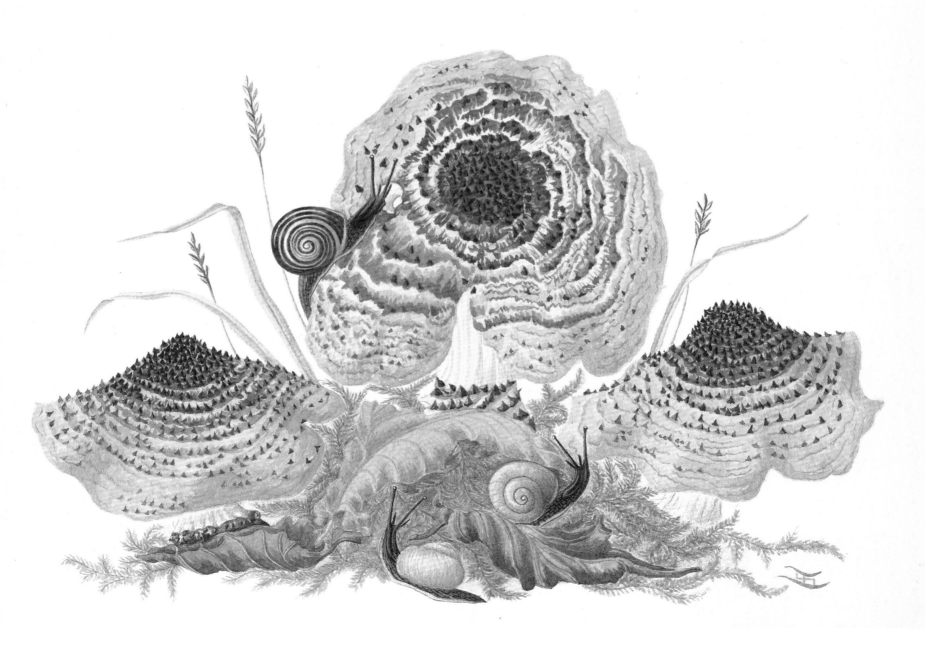

Inocybe bongardii
looking as if finely carved out of wood, it
grew under spruce and is singular in its
lovely muted green and faint pink glow.

Micromphale species
delightful small people but smelling strongly of garlic. Their relative Marasmius
scorodonius is used as a substitute garlic flavouring.

Hygrophoropsis aurantiaca
apricot and rose-coral throughout, it was
treasure-trove shining against a carpet of fir
needles as if with a light of its own.

Pleurotus cornucopiae
found by lucky chance when I went to buy sweet peas for my mother. They grew on a
heavy oak log, in a small family wood-yard, and were a problem for both car and studio.
In full beauty and varying forms and shades they returned for many autumns.

Cystoderma granulosa
came up under a noble fir-tree in an array of
every age and size, all with small stockinged
feet, yet each one a distinct personality.

Mycena acicola
dainty and fragile, they were from the generous wood-pile in the garden where
they favoured small pieces of branch shaded from the sun.

Lepista flaccida
was growing in a heap of old branches lying in
grass beside a larch-wood, the graceful shapes
and golden-brown colour a delight to the eye.

Inocybe geophylla var. lilacina
appeared in a flock on a shady bank where the
exquisite lilac showed well against the fresh fall
of spruce needles. Like some others of the
family it is poisonous, perhaps even to animals,
for I have never found Inocybes eaten away.

Amanita aspera var. valida
it was found only twice in solitary grace, on
earth banks under beeches and quite ravishing
with the loveliness of grey and white and a
dancing form. Two of the painted group were
successive stages of one toadstool.

Collybia peronata
a delicious toadstool, rosy fawn in cap and,
when fresh as dew, with the most captivating
lemon yellow fluffy feet.

Coprinus filiformis
of a delicate frailty that needed much tender care on the
way to my work-table.

Mycena haematopus
extremely fragile, this endearing little
concourse needed utmost attention on the
journey home, for each toadstool is filled with
ruby water and, if broken, is drained of colour
to lie limp and ghost-like in one's hand.

Pleurotus ostreatus

of which this shows only a few of the fascinating tiers of light indigo, lined with delicate pink gills, which climbed the splendid beech trunk of one of many lovely old trees at Longleat later destroyed by the great hurricane. The Pleurotus here is quite different from the small beige commercial ones sold in shops, which proves the advantage of being wild.

Lenzites saepiaria
on whose burnt orange fans its own personal
moss grew, fine as silk velvet and with the
same delicious feel.

Tubaria conspersa
another variation on the conspersa theme as on page 20, these with silken rather
than woolly feet.

Bulgaria inquinans
was growing all over a young fallen oak from
which a section was sawn to take home. The
youthful cups were so highly polished inside
that they reflected the blue sky with the
bewitching effect of tiny pieces of sky
scattered all over the wood.

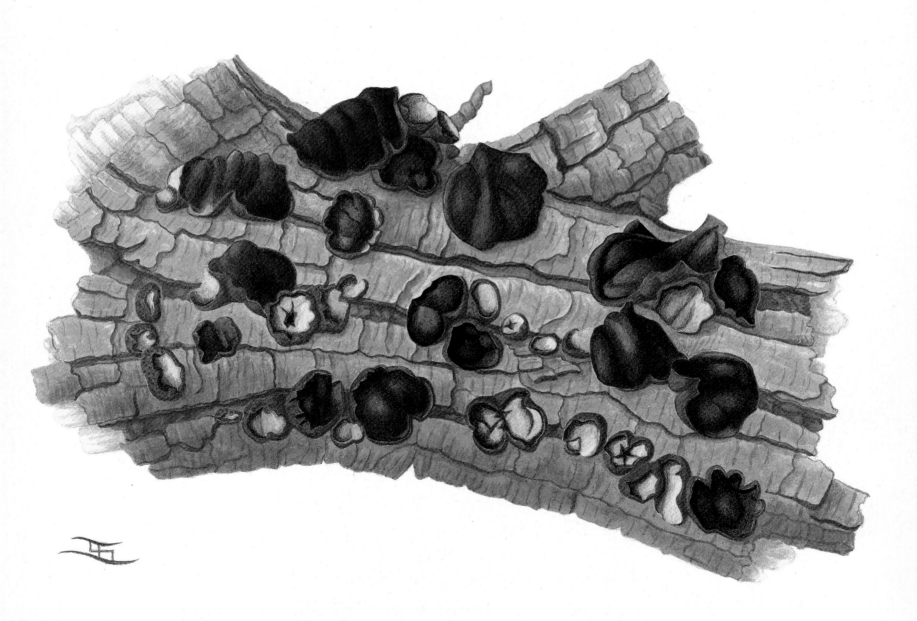

Pholiota mutabilis
painted in the richness of the moist caps which
were a luscious golden chestnut, for they dry
to a fawn colour of less impact and charm.

Stereum hirsutum
was a piece only of the six-foot fallen trunk
where grew range upon range of small
undulating shelves in brilliant gold and red
orange. The whole display was spectacular.

Xylaria polymorpha
this curious coral-like growth with such an
unusual and exquisite colouring appeared on
a pear-tree stump and remained unidentified
when shown to several experts. It was very
firm but pure velvet to the touch, the brown
corkscrew base being inside the wood.

Lycogala epidendrum
a retiring little creature found by reason of the minute daily garden search.

Xylaria polymorpha
two years later the mysterious coral above
repaid my steady patience by springing into
enthusiastic growth to become this being of
extraordinary shapes and texture.

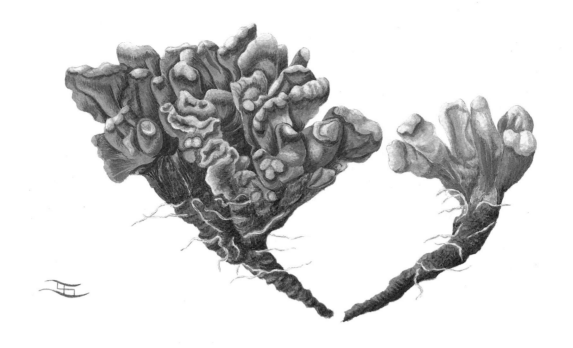

Armillaria polymyces
the only ones for which there was time before the gorgeous multitude of great golden
toadstools, mounting row after row up a huge chestnut-tree stump, disappeared never to return.

Coprinus radians
was also a single toadstool growing on an
earth-covered wall under hawthorn. Different
views of its charming gold head, and sizes as it
grew, gave a complete picture of its character.

Bovista nigrescens
a great annoyance to golfers of former times in its young golf-ball look-alike stage
before the fascinating patterns began.

Schleroderma verrucosum
found only once under a large oak and was of
a complexity of colour glazing and detail to try
the most patient, yet worth every minute for
the splendour of its rich deep gold and
contrasting dark violet-sepia spores and lining.

Russula atrorubens
this bright scarlet form is one of the most brilliant
of this family which could lend its colours to the
radiance of stained glass windows.

Boletus (Xerocomus) fragrans
grew in grass beside an oak wood and had a
perfume of fruit. The splendid crimson stalk
narrowed underground to a deeply buried
root-like base.

Physarum species
looking like coral pearled with dew, it was
growing on an almost disintegrating alder tree
lying in the marsh, a gathering and fixing
after the 'tadpole' phase of myxomycetes
described in the text. The white underside
was unbelievably soft and delicate.

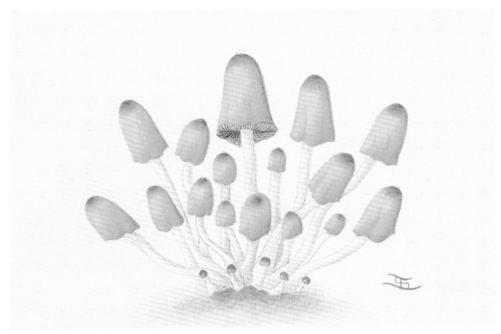

Coprinus cothumatus
this adorable and transient apricot-coloured toadstool has a predilection for warm
greenhouses or cellars. This family came up between the flagstones near the
central-heating boiler at a friend's house.

Pulchericium caeruleum
found by a friend on the under side of an old
piece of ash bean-prop, rare in Britain, more
frequent in southern Europe, but much
prefers the tropics and sub-tropics. As seen
here it colours the wood on which it grows.

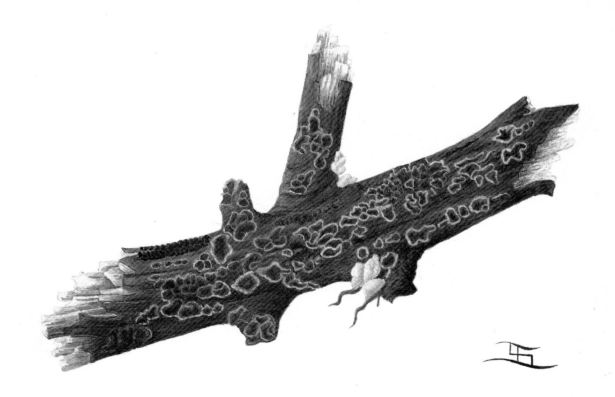

Tricholomopsis rutilans var. variegata
grew on an old pine stump in a satisfactory succession of ages, from the very smallest, looking
perfect on the grey-green wood and was another which demanded glazes and much patience.

Boletus (Xerocomus) pulverulentus
adds to its impressive colours by turning
peacock blue when bruised or cut, then grey-
green as on the cap. Found in thin grass
under beech trees and later in a mossy
hollow by firs.

Cordiceps militaris
a small carnivorous creature growing on a buried caterpillar or chrysalis for choice.

Tremella mesenterica with
Coryne sarcoides
needs wet weather to be in full golden glory:
dried it is a shrivelled orange body but
revives in rain. The purple Coryne grew
harmoniously with it on an old apple branch.

Daedaleopsis rufescens
on the low trunk of a very old New Zealand
Hebe, it was too fascinating in colour and
form ever to come back again.

Lactarius fulvissimus
growing under ancient beeches it glowed
unbelievably in the evening sunlight, an
intensity of colour almost impossible to paint,
let alone print, and needing glazes of gold,
scarlet lake and burnt sienna.

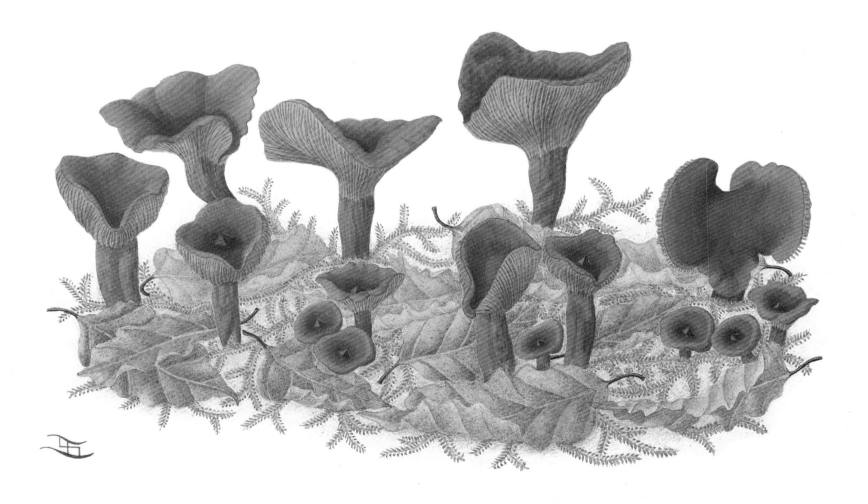

Collybia fusipes
entirely fascinating in rich depth of colour,
convoluted base and variety of shapes in the
little top-knotted heads. It grew in burnt ground
where a stand of oak had been cut and 'tidied'.

Pluteus cinereofuscus
was found under lilac, unusual and with a most attractive pattern of crazing on the
caps due to its circular cell structure.

Amanita spissa brown form
the smaller of two marvels living beneath
mighty beeches; the other had been fifteen
inches across but was beaten down by one
who did not love toadstools.

Megacollybia platyphylla
statuesque and imposing, this beauty grew tall above her shapely companions on an
antique beech stump, all their caps adorned, where the pure white gills showed, with a
border of finest lace.

Inocybe lanuginosa
another with the fine woodcarving look, it
grew on the borders of spruce and birch by
the sphagnum moss marsh.

Mycena oortiana
tough and persistent, regenerating in water after being dried out, it is a small
individual of original imagination in form.

Paxillus involutus
in the same place as the Inocybe but it is
catholic in its tastes, inhabiting mixed woods
and varying markedly in size and colour,
though always the same graceful shape.

Pholiota confragosa
in 1977 I was told that this had been found in
that year by only one other person for the first
time in thirty years; certainly I have not found
its rich colours and charming shapes again.

Russula fellea
found growing in a family under beech trees, it
was the one with a perfume of violets, at other
times a scent of fruit with a hint of the sea.

Lepiota fuscovinacea
is a rare toadstool which nevertheless came to
my garden, appearing happily under a venerable
gooseberry bush which attacked me with ferocity
when I wanted to collect my exquisitely
patterned model. It is very poisonous.

Tephrocybe palustris
a name sounding like a Greek goddess for one of the unconsidered but so lovely
small inhabitants of the sphagnum bog.

Psalliota campestris
how often can we see these tender pristine
gills of the wild mushroom when all those in
the shops are old before their time with gills
of dark dull brown.

Mycena species
(left) from the garden wood-pile,
an unassuming but exquisite
toadstool perfect in restrained grace.

Clitocybe species
(right) each one was solitary,
growing among old holly leaves,
and nearby on a twig was the tiny
Dacrymyces deliquescens.

Crinipellis stipitaria
grew under lilac and were so appealing in their singular shapes and colouring.

Psathyrella obtusata
(left) delightful little Vietnamese
hats, with silken feet enclosing the
minute infants, these were at
home on a fallen branch.

Mycena polygramma
(right) again the wood-pile, an
inexhaustible source of charming
lesser toadstools in great variety.

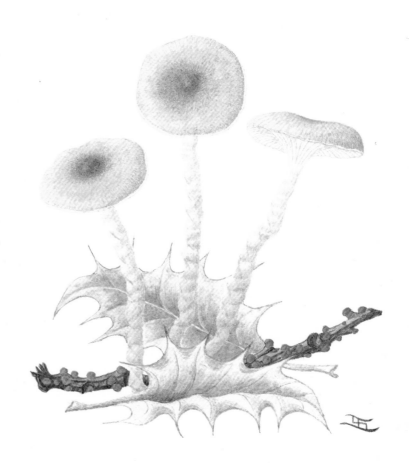

Calocera viscosa
(*left*) can come up on buried roots
or surface pieces of wood all over
the forest floor like delicate
tongues of flame.

Lepiota cristata
(*right*) appeared in mossy ground
under a Bramley apple which this
delicate toadstool seems to favour
as its companion tree.

Galerina pseudopumila
an enchanting small person with soft
plush feet and almost transparent
collarettes.

Mycena species
(*left*) was found twice, only on the
dead wood at the base of
Rosa Maigold.

Coriolus versicolor
(*right*) on a piece of fir, was a
small edition of the red-brown form
of this decorative bracket fungus.

Amanita rubescens

the beech leaves were removed gently to find a treasure-house beneath of young toadstools, from the smallest rosy infants through steady growth to the splendour of the mature adult, whose rich patterning looked like Persian brocade. This was a group such as I have not found since: that day there was no rain to wash away the lovely decoration.

Coprinus romagnesianus
another of the more than two hundred kinds I found in my half-acre garden it was a lovely toadstool, slender and elegant, with a host of cream-coloured children, growing at the foot of an aged oak post.

Coprinus truncorum
this family is unending in its variety of graceful and transient small parasols.

Coprinus romagnesianus
a case to prove the imaginative diversity of form and colour toadstools give us for our joy, and often as a puzzle to solve, this silver beauty grew three years later from the same mycelium in the same place as its companion on the page.

Lepista nuda

with fluted chalices of enchanting colours, these were a unique find for me and were growing under a monkey-puzzle tree at Longleat. This both engaging and edible toadstool varies greatly in shape, colour and size according to the weather and its chosen tree which can be broad-leaved or conifer. Its edibility depends on being certain of the identity and only when cooked.

Psatbyrella arata

this sometimes modest family,
always of entrancing shapeliness,
has many delightful members,
often with mauve or grey-purple
gills and here with a cap edged in
pale lilac.

Dacrymyces stillatus and Coryne sarcoides
a lovable little piece of branch ornamented with amethyst and gold.

Psatbyrella gracilis

another with the same faultless
poise, dark grey when wet, but
when dry had a faint flush of rose
and gold with soft grey at the cap
edge. The young ones are a
complete contrast.

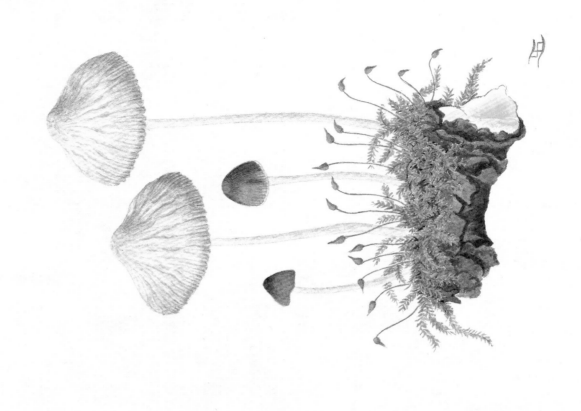

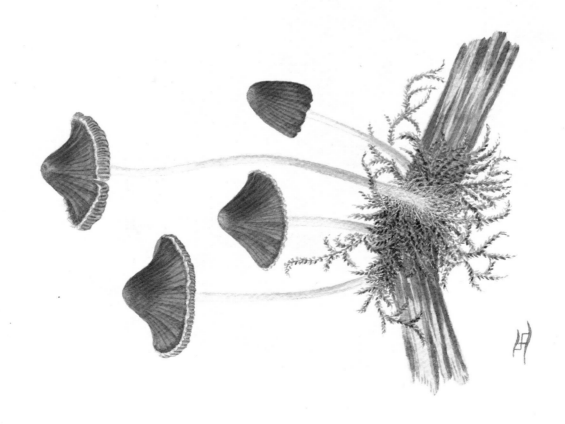

Lactarius blennius

was a complete delight to paint. The soft green, reminiscent of the pebbles on the holy island of Iona, combined with an embroidery of deep wine red, kept my sense of wonder and affection alive during many hours of work. The minute infant looks as if it could never achieve the intricacy and colour of the full-grown loveliness.

Inocybe petiginosa
a lovable relative which also found a home under the same trees: perhaps both relate particularly to the apple.

Tephrocybe tesquorum
was found nestling in a hollow birch stump, filled with fir needles, in the sphagnum moss marsh.

Inocybe fastigiata
was comfortable in moss under my apple trees. It is dangerously poisonous which in no way detracts from its charm.

Entoloma nidorosum

in my mother's garden where hedgehogs had slept the winter before in a thick nest of leaves, it produced a remarkable individual with a sumptuous formation of rosy gills, from which the spores fell colouring its neighbour's cap with a coral glow. Lovely but not to be eaten.

Boletus calopus
strong, yet with a flow of movement as if hastening eagerly forward, the rift in its noble stalk and the marks of a squirrel's meal showed the tender colours beneath the latticed surface. It grew in a grassy clearing near beech trees.

Lactarius mitissimus
grew among spruce needles near the sphagnum marsh. Its gills were rose-ivory, perfect with the copper-orange cap.

Boletus (Tylopilus) felleus
growing in woods, is a worthy companion, strong yet alluring in the harmony of chestnut brown, pink and soft fawn. Too bitter to eat.

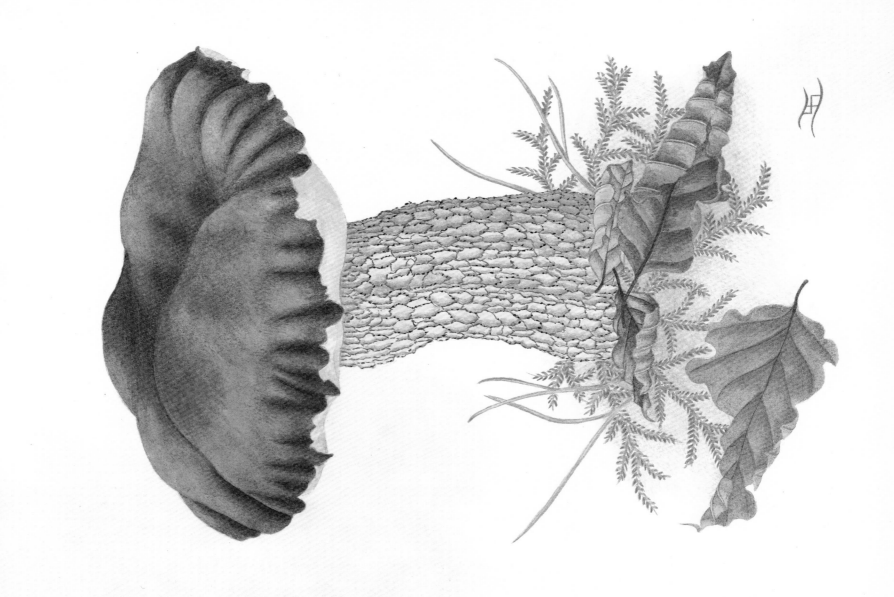

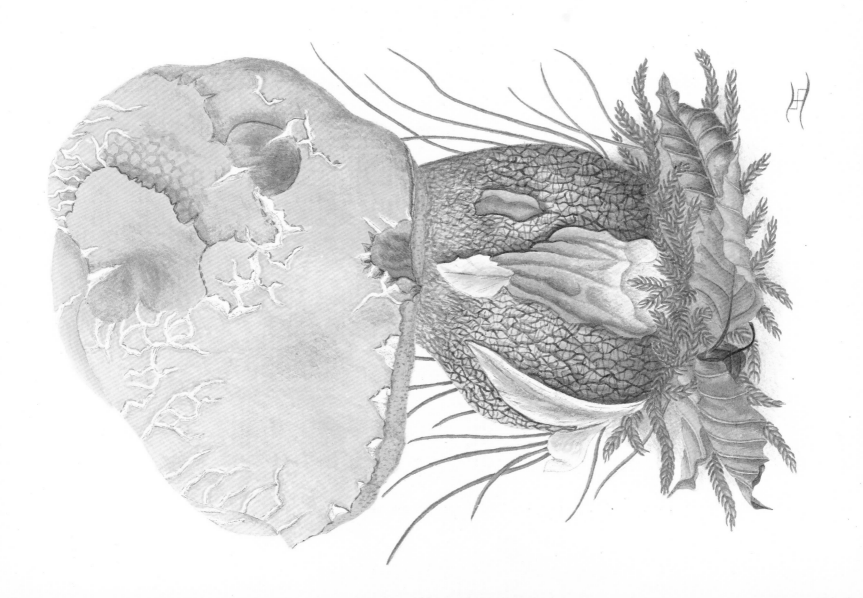

Morchella conica

uniquely fascinating in complex form, also edible, this member of an intriguing group grew suddenly, as is the way of toadstools, in the middle of an inhospitable stony path between an old apple tree and a rhododendron beside my dust-bin.

Coprinus micaceus

the delicacy of colour as it appeared in first freshness in the shade of an old filbert bush was as captivating as the variety of small heads.

Peziza succosa

a small ballet company which danced at the base of a privet hedge.

Coprinus sylvaticus

another of this delightful family, one with fly-away heads and the infants looking very like those of micaceus - but they aren't. If in doubt, give them an hour or so to grow.

Russula Mairei

a brilliant and crowded array grew under ancient beech trees lighting up the shadowy ground with scarlet. The smallest ones beneath the leaves are pure white. The Russulas excel in enamelled colours.

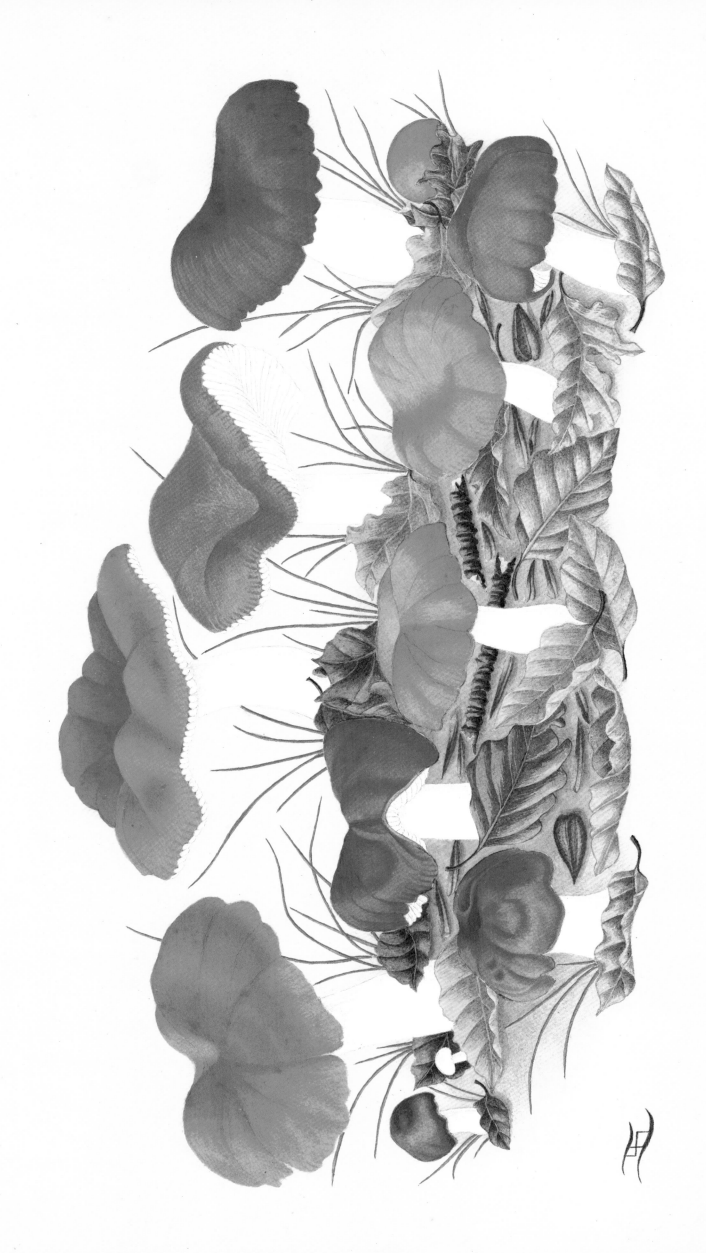

Lepiota clypeolaria
was on ivy-covered ground by the
gate and had an unpretentious but
very elegant appearance.

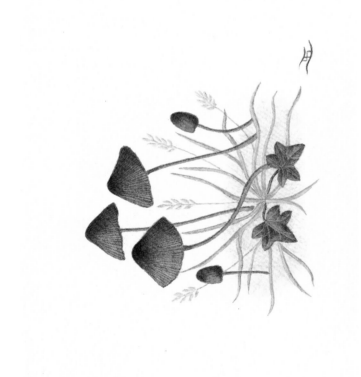

Psathyrella species
simple but of delicate modest charm.

Pholiota ochroleuca
grew on a buried bush root on a
bank, in colour restrained and as
if carved out of ivory.

Phaeolus Schweinitzii

can be a large layered bracket often growing on the base of a tree trunk, or as these on an old buried conifer stump, with the same magnificent colours of the velvet caps but with the added fascination of rich brown and olive-green stalks. The caps and stalks developed so gently that as they grew they clasped the blades of grass, not bending one.

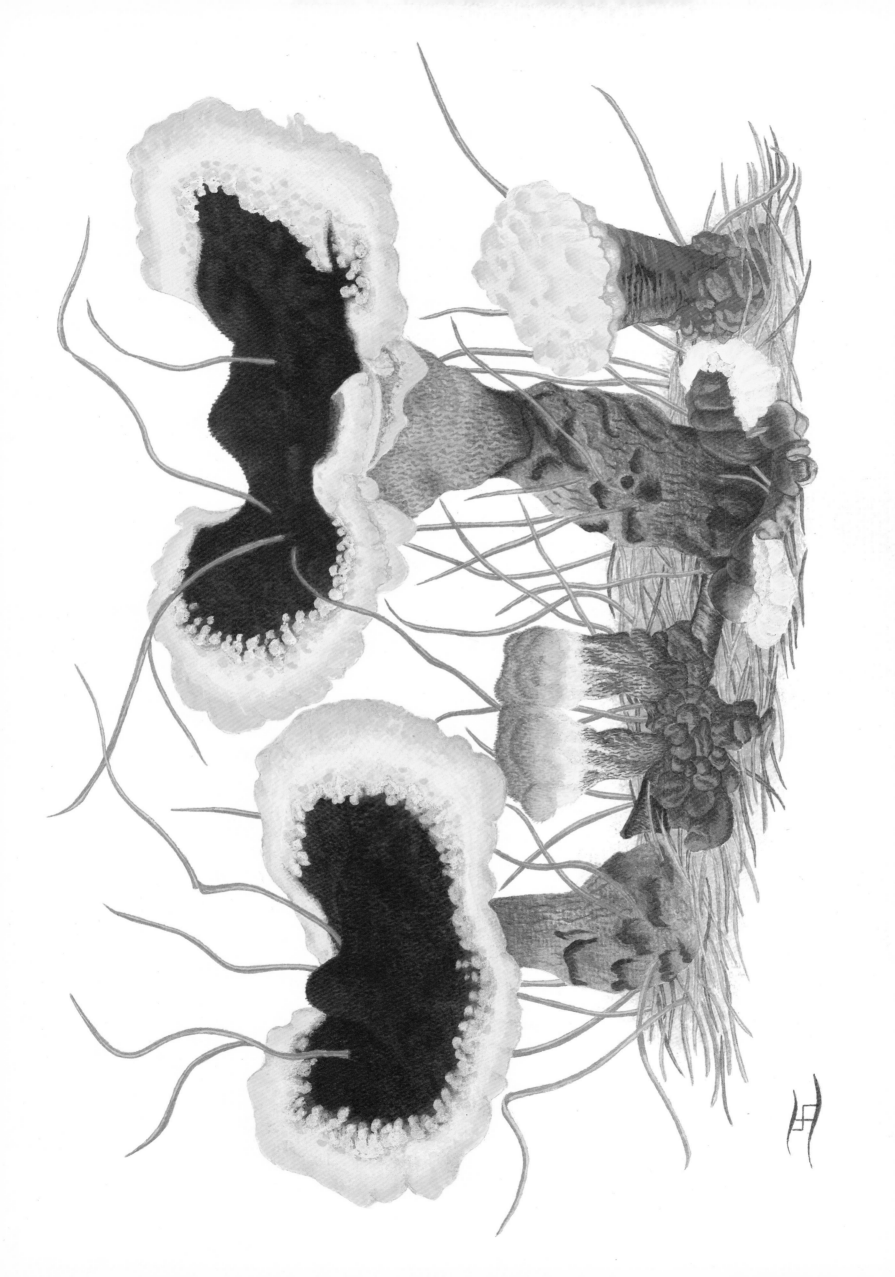

Boletus (Tubiporus) luridus
supposed to grow in woods but
these splendid creatures came to
wait for me in a grassy bank
beside my small gate. Work
began at once for in two hours
the golden stem and scarlet
vermilion pores were fading, a
state in which this brilliant
toadstool is often pictured.
Growing round it, and identified
by an expert, was a very
interesting Selaginella, or club
moss, species.

Boletus (Ixocomus) elegans
a very proper name for such
graceful growth and attitude. This
toadstool likes larch trees and
these had come to a young
plantation to live.

Lactarius rufus
a small version of the same toadstool as on page 21, it seems, which is surprising.

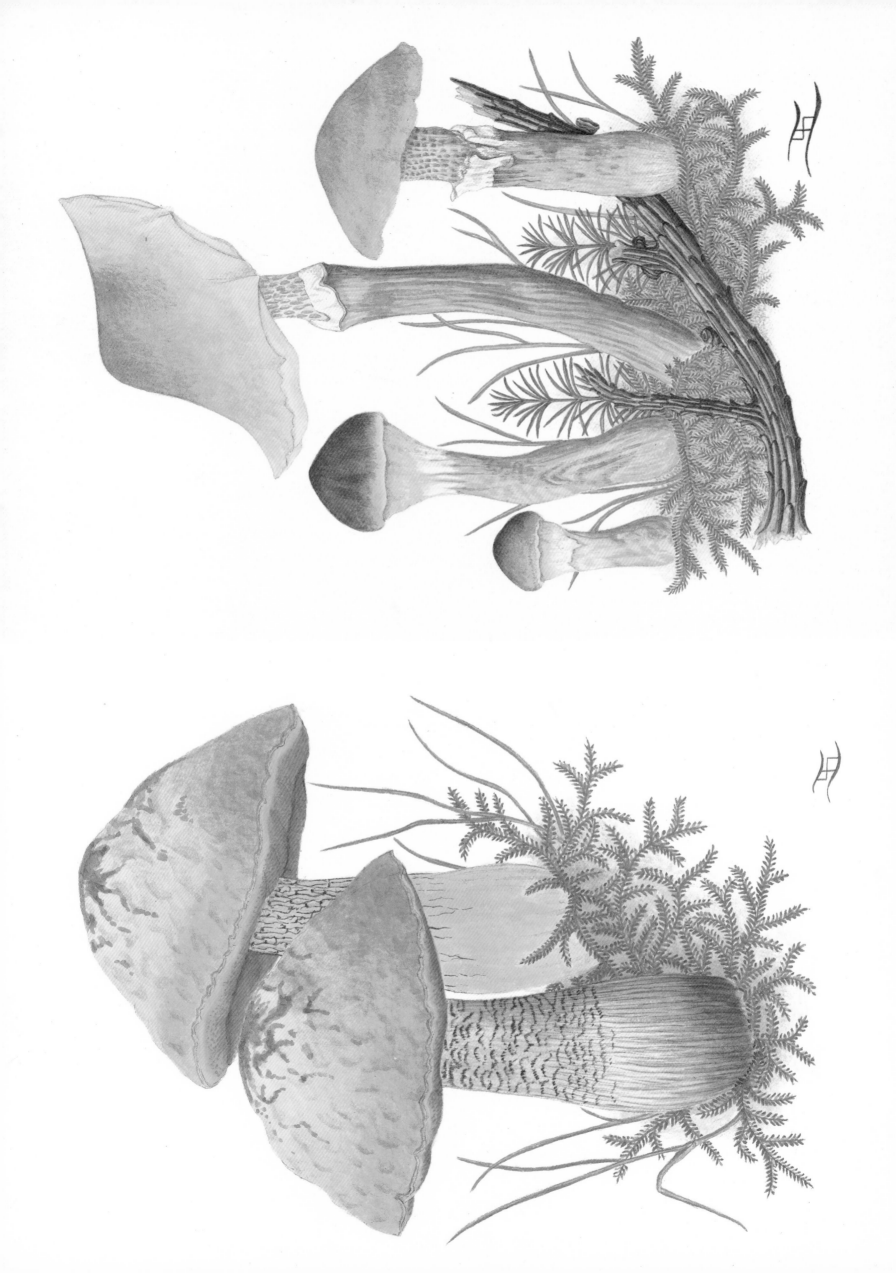

Geastrum triplex

looking below a large filbert at a pile of leaves I was astonished by these cream stars lying before me. Swiftest action again, for very soon the "petals" turn under and the silken surface is broken by deep cracks when the centre is raised, as if on feet, so that the spores get a head start. In rain, as each drop falls on the sphere, a tiny puff of spores, like smoke, blows out into the wind.

Byerkandera adusta
unspectacular but quietly attractive with its variety of soft browns and the frilled white-lined fans ornamenting an old oak post.

Coprinus disseminatus
these arrive in innumerable companies on ground where dead roots lie buried, old wood with bark on it, or even on mossy stones. They cluster in all sizes, their entrancing pale gold heads turning later to soft grey - a lifetime in three or four days. Well suited, they appear in one corner of my garden every fortnight through summer and autumn. This year they have decided to climb, which is new to me, and are crowding in thousands up five feet of the large trunk of a dead apple tree.

Cyatbus olla
grew on an old piece of privet like a collection of humming birds' nests with the "eggs" not that much smaller. Once more, when the friendly rain falls on them, a drop will shoot out a small spore-filled globe.

Boletus (Xerocomus) subtomentosus

again such fortune in finding this handsome and impressive example of its kind, supported by two less unusual members of the family. Some crack into the most fascinating designs and when younger have a pearled edge to the cap.

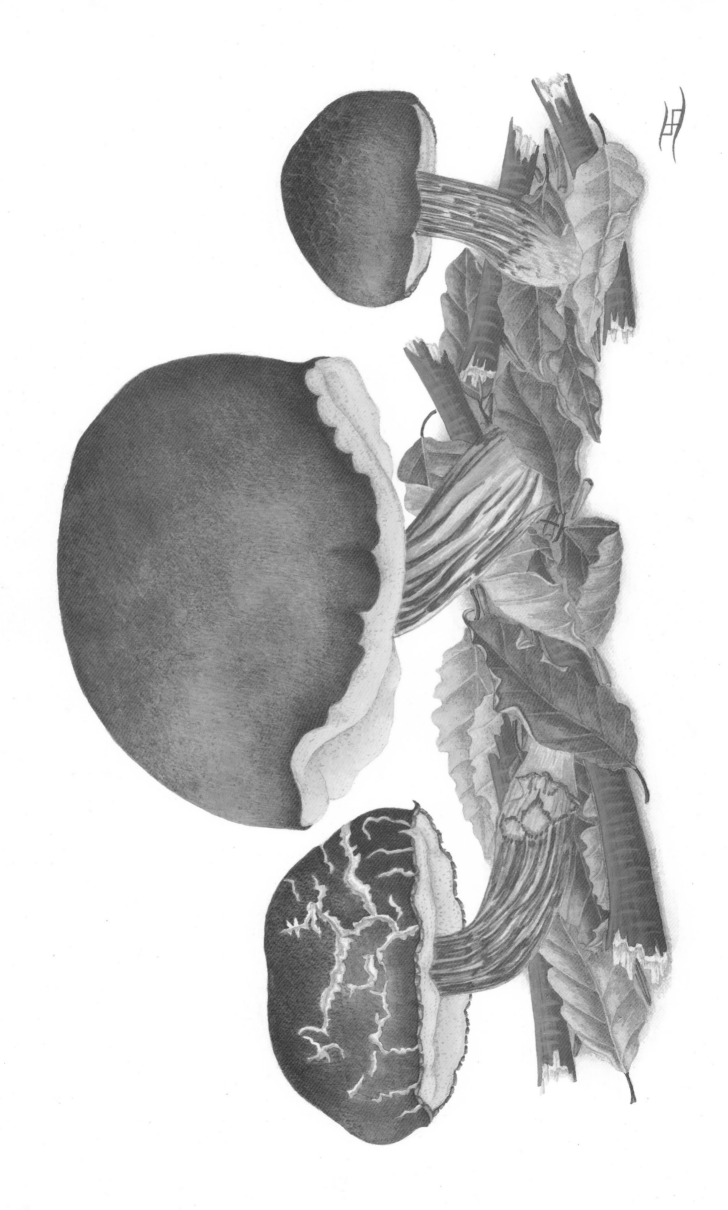

Agrocybe paludosa
most fascinating in shapes, colours
and enchanting speckled and
banded stalks - a captivating group.

Agrocybe paludosa
a small form of the more opulent relation on the opposite page. To the artist they
look quite different!

Stropharia semiglobata
animals are necessary to this
graceful toadstool for, like roses,
to it manure is manna.

Psalliota sylvatica

came up in flocks, years running, under the large filbert, delighting me with their ravishing pink gills, of consummate delicacy, under soft brown and grey caps.

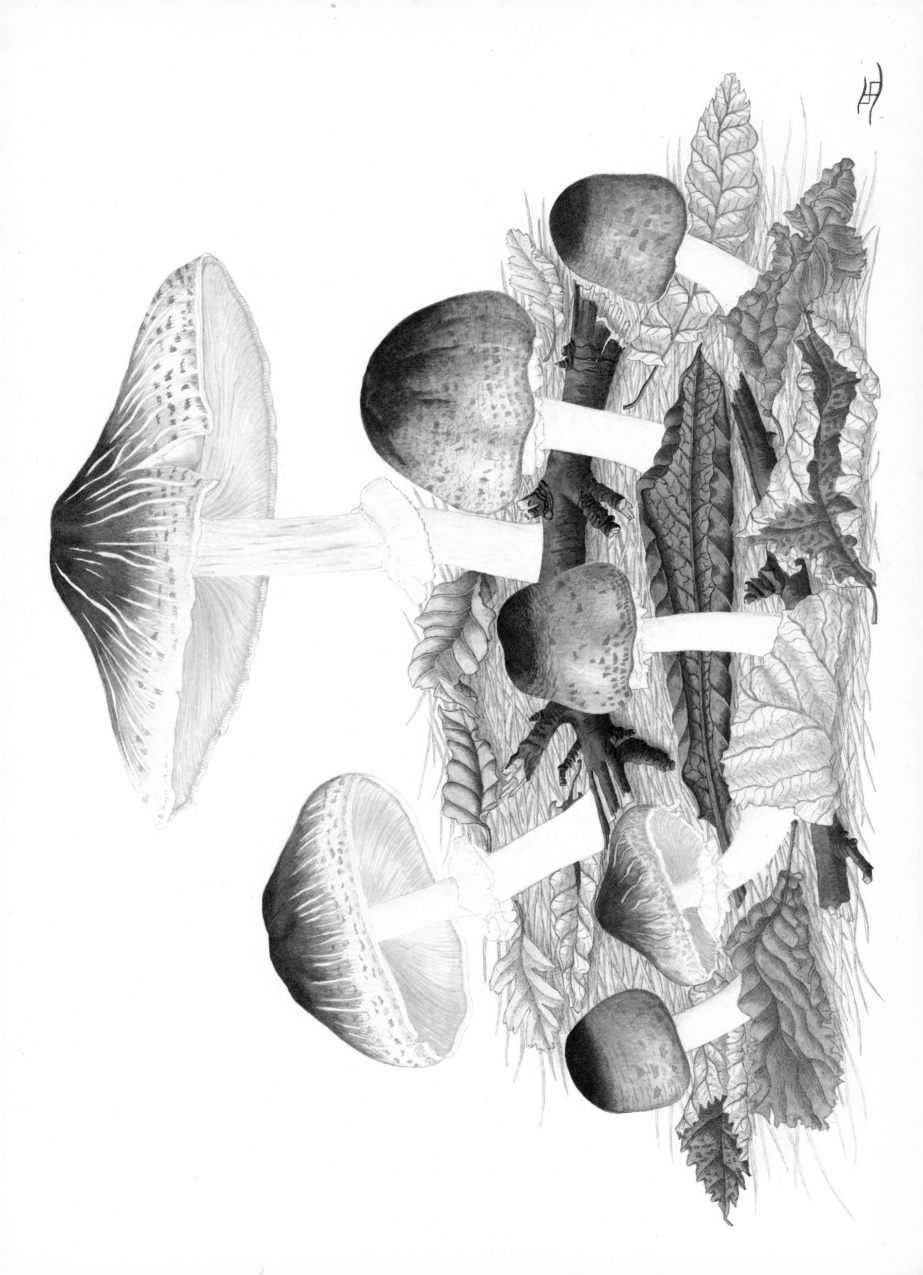

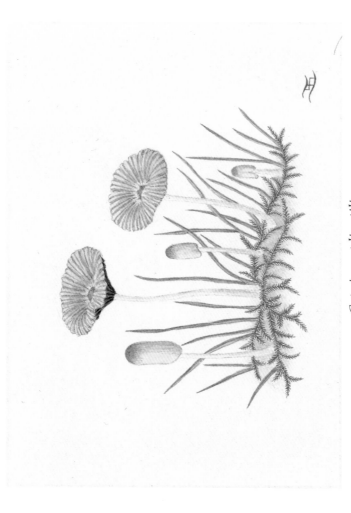

Coprinus plicatilis
Solitary and very fragile, it is painted as a collection to show its stages through life.

Amanita pantherina
from dove grey to fawn and sepia,
all combined with silver-white,
this being is perfect in elegance.
It is too beautiful, apart from
being very poisonous, to eat.

Psathyrella conopilea
found in damp ground near my
mature and fruitful wood-pile, it is
of a more slender and fragile
grace, but the perfect companion
for the Amanita.

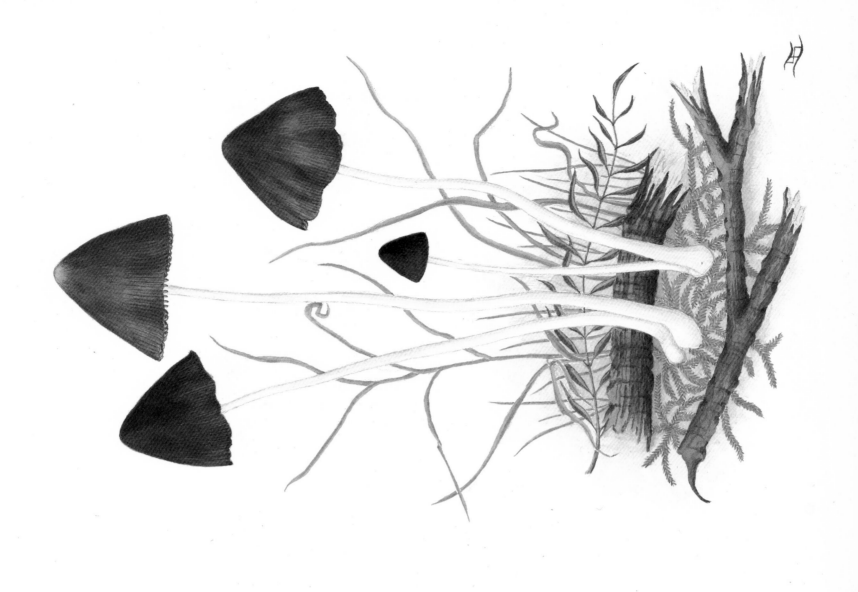

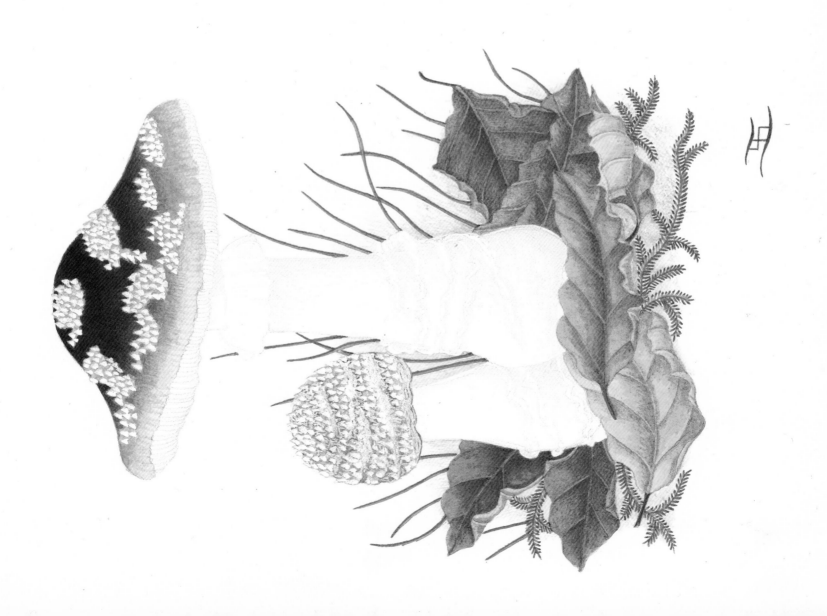

Clitocybe nebularis

an exercise in the loveliness of subdued colour and the deeply satisfying perfection of line and form, these beauties were found growing in many fascinating shapes and sizes in a fairy circle by the roadside.

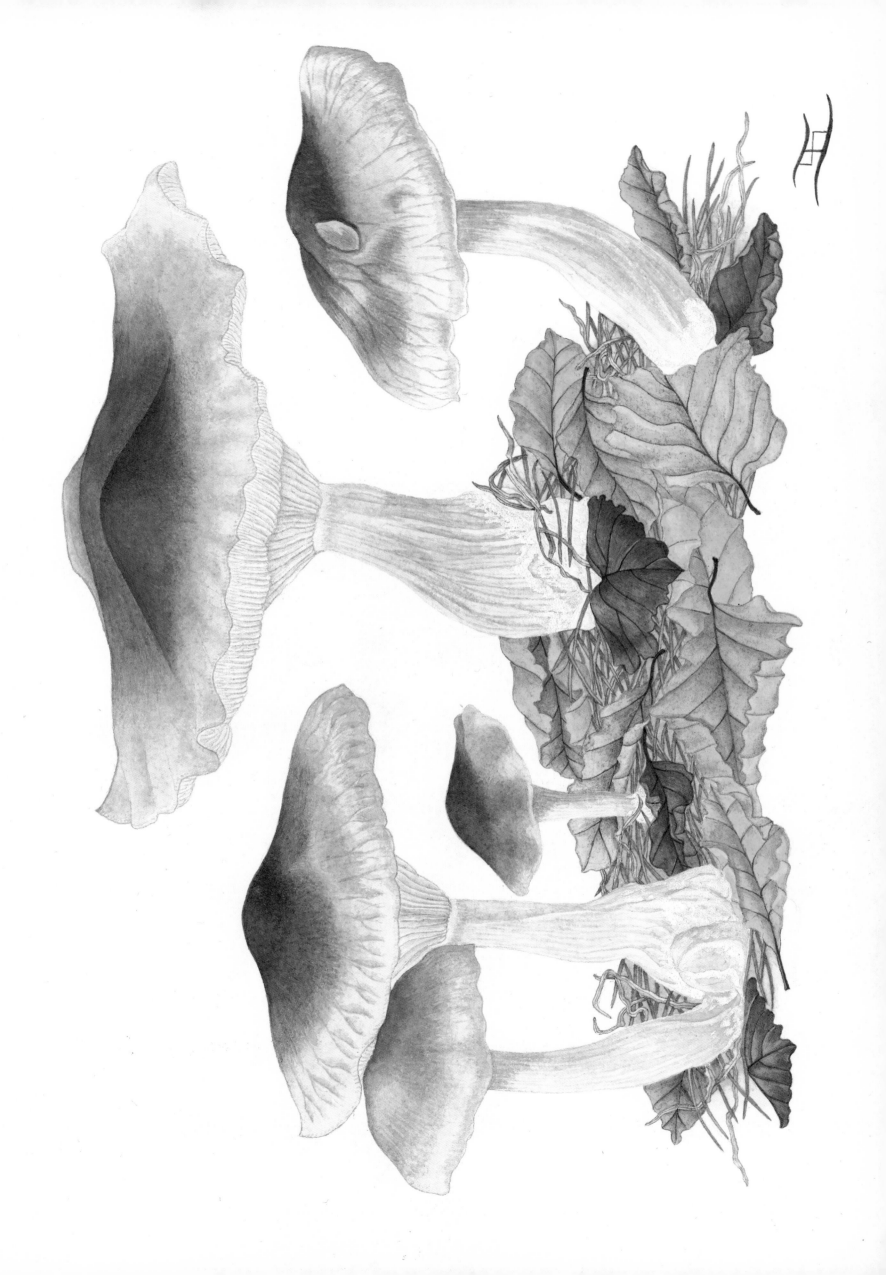

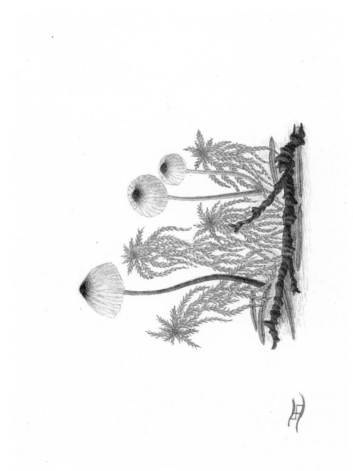

Mycena galopus
gentle, unassuming and so appealing in their quiet modesty.

Clitocybe geotropa
contrasted becomingly with the fallen leaves in an oak wood clearing near a spruce.

Tremellodon gelatinosum
with a bloom like untouched plums and small translucent white points beneath, it needed great care in the gathering from where it grew on the large spruce stump of a tree cut down many years ago.

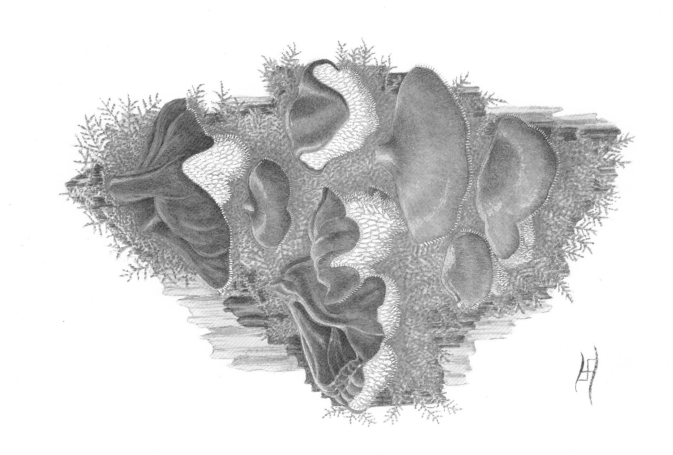

Phallus impudicus

giving off an undoubtedly dreadful smell, it is nevertheless a creature of great beauty looking
as if carved out of green and white jades. The syrup on the caps is greatly loved by flies.

Tricholomopsis rutilans
aptly named as it is indeed
rutilant, rutile being red oxide of
titanium which presumably glows.
It grew in solitary splendour.

Imocybe flocculosa
not common, it came up under my filbert which seemed to welcome many guests.

Pluteus cervinus
an entrancing harmony of brown,
dusky pink and ivory, it appeared
on an old beech stump and can
also be a warm grey.

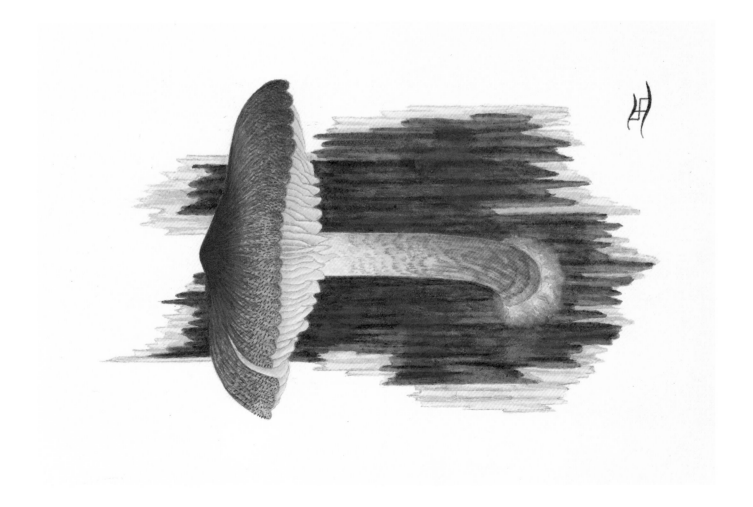

Boletus (Tubiporus) regius

a gorgeous rarity which grew in numbers under a magnificent beech tree - so rare that they are trying to protect it as an endangered species. Its colours of purple and gold are beyond what one might imagine. The love-bird green from the pressure of handling turned back to gold after forty minutes. Where mice came to supper they uncovered both first and second underlayers, rich crimson and then gold. A magical toadstool.

Amanita citrina

bewitching in its ethereal, iridescent colour making it look luminous and almost translucent. It grew between a noble oak and a great larch, a piece of ground where a most interesting variety of toadstools found a congenial home, a border-line for larch and oak lovers where they grew together. The owner did promise not to cut these trees down.

Gnomes without a name

they grew on an ancient wooden seed box, a most engaging mystery.

Amanita rubescens

this unusual and beautiful golden form of a both lovely and edible toadstool was growing, as is its habit, under beech trees.

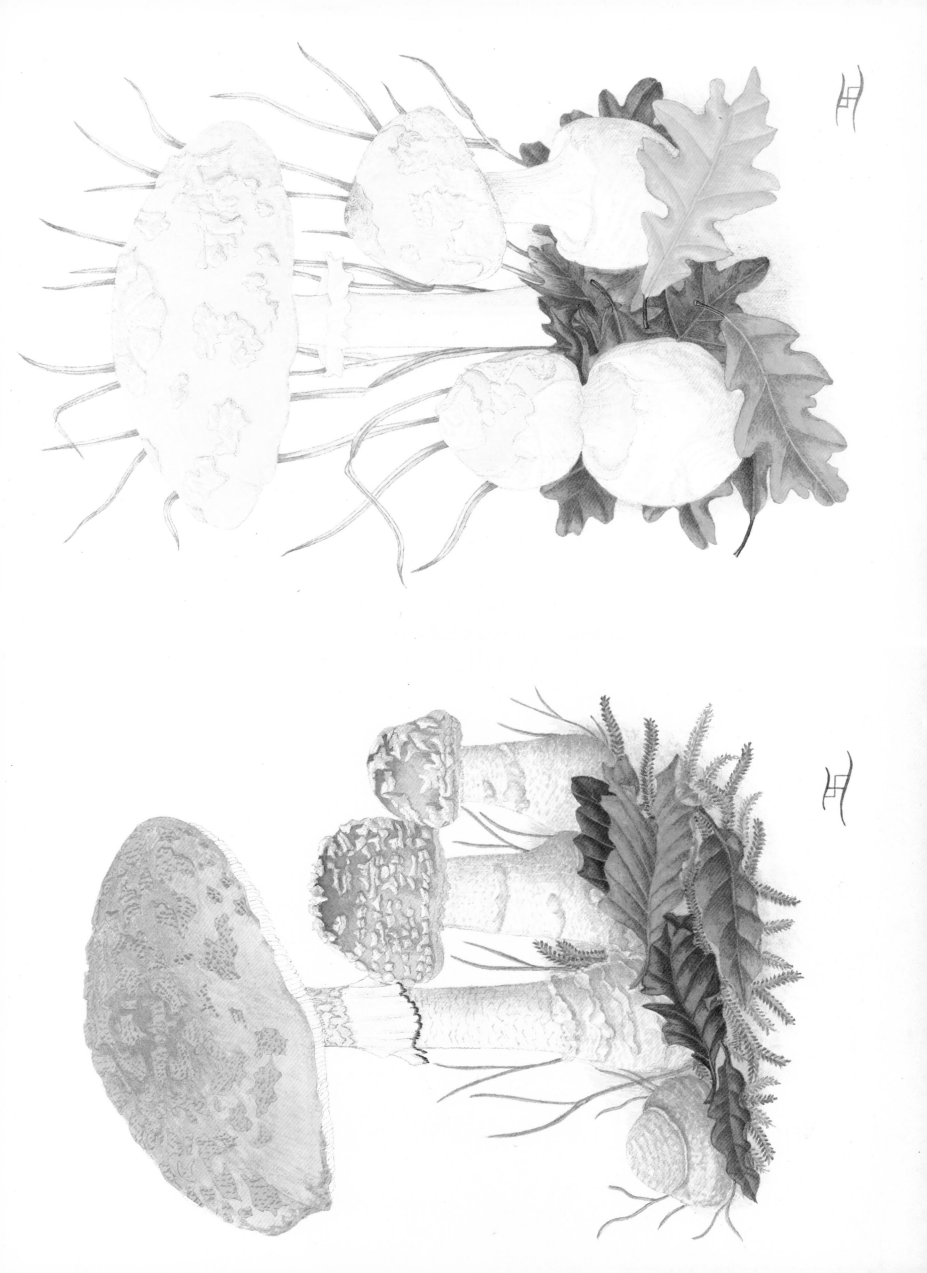

Tricholoma ustale
a stream of every age and size flowed down a bank, deeply strewn with beech leaves, making the ground glow with rich colour.

Collybia species
resembling Collybia distorta in the twisted stems, the burnished sienna-gold caps, emphasized by a delicate ribbon of paler colour round the edge, make this smaller toadstool very attractive. It grew only beside old bracken stalks near conifers.

Laccaria species
small but of much character, it grew on conifer wood lying in wet sphagnum moss.

Hypholoma fasciculare
these have a genius for growing into delicate sculptural groups most pleasing to one's sense of line and colour, but not of taste.

Cortinarius largus

how did creation manage this exquisite creature in all its beauty of soft cream, tender flax-blue, copper and translucent pearl, combined with a most graceful carriage and all against the background of shining autumn beech leaves. There were many and I lingered a long time standing among such a lovely gathering.

Pholiota myosotis

green is uncommon in toadstools, most fascinating in this chrysoprase colour and with the wonderful finishing touch of ash-grey infants.

Galerina paludosa

another small treasure which decorated the sphagnum marsh, where I spent so many happy hours, with its pretty caps and appealing stripy stalks.

Pustularia catina

grew among sticks on the boundary of my nice area of not-to-be-disturbed piles of wood and debris.

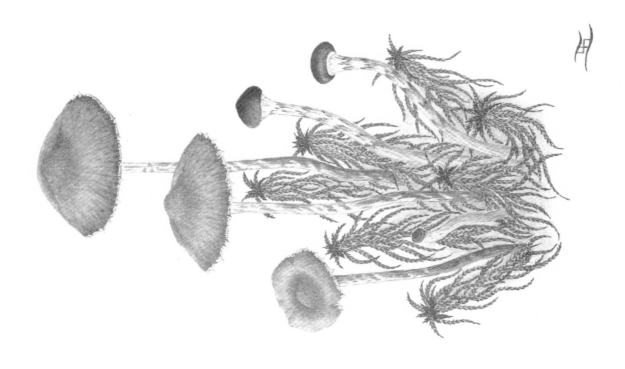

Schleroderma citrinum

grew on a fern trunk near conifers; near birch it is nearly white, under beech palest gold, but wherever it may be found it is often delightfully patterned as with little flowers.

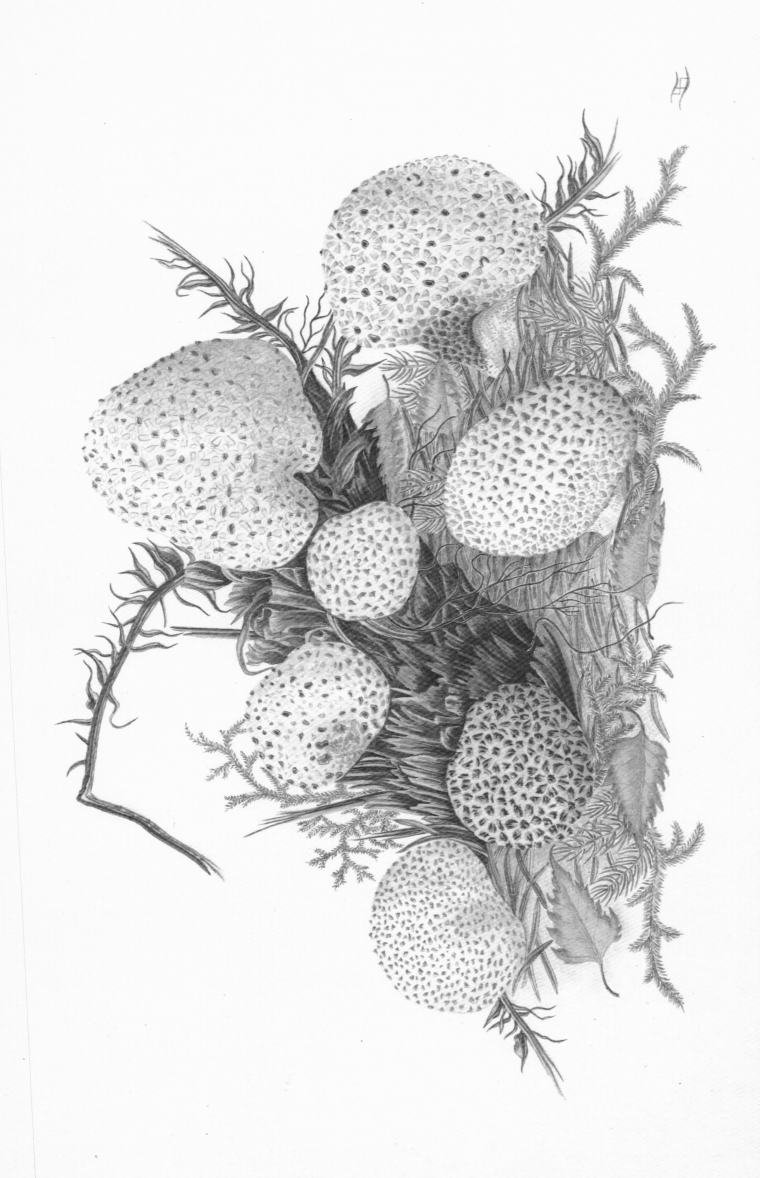

Armillaria mellea
of great charm and a bad, not
always deserved, reputation.
Another family member has
become famous as the greatest
living organism on earth for which
such a group looks far too small,
being only a part of the whole.

Lepiota fulvella
another touching small family group from my garden, as so often each one with a
minute character of its own.

Collybia velutipes
suddenly made their captivating
appearance all over oak logs
stored in a friend's cellar. Much
larger out-of-doors, but these still
have the lovely apricot caps and
dark velvet feet of their kind.

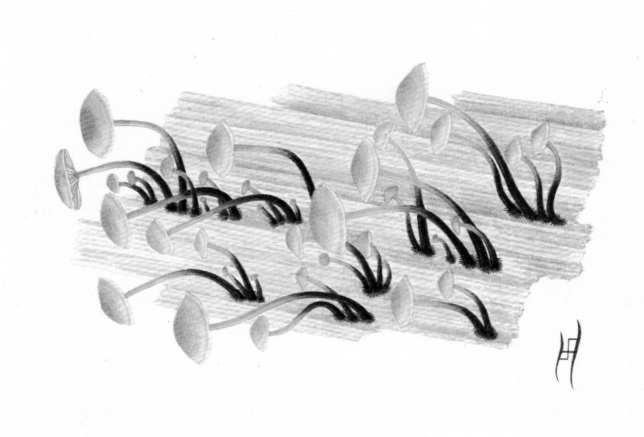

Coprinus lagopus
(top) difficult to keep up with as it moved all the time. It was to be treated with great gentleness as the whole structure depended on the clear water filling the stem: punctured it collapsed completely.

Psathyrella jerdonii
(lower) on a day of mist and rain in bridal dress, drying to a more ordinary little brown person, but in water-laden air it was covered in white lace, the cap festooned with delicate scallops and points.

Coprinus species
(top) The unknown which grew so fast that the single infant had to be painted every two hours to create this picture of its life story.

Coprinus disseminatus
(lower) appealing in adorable crowds, this is the later colour of those on page 101.

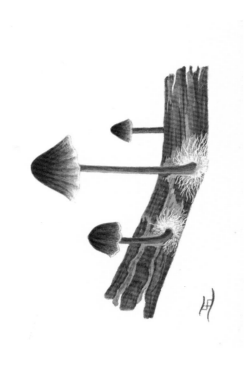

Mycena leucogala
a charming small creature with gossamer feet.

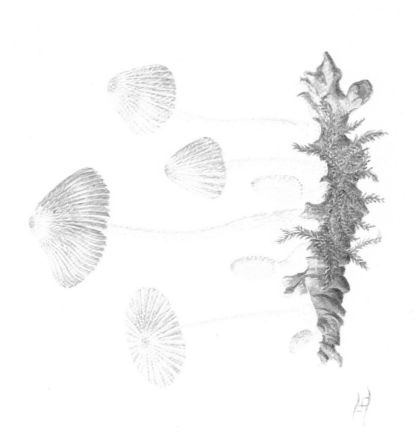

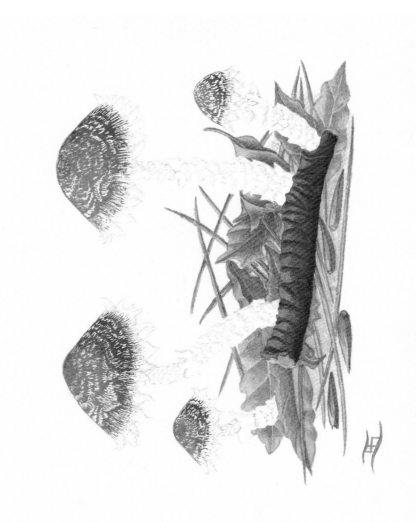

136

Coprinus galericuliformis
(*top*) each of the demure and at first glance much-alike little members of this large family is, nevertheless, its own particular self and so to be painted.

Panaeolina foenisecii
(*lower*) has an engaging allotment of colour to each age from the emerging infant in gold to the elegant warm grey of the grown-ups.

Tubaria furfuracea
a small unconsidered inhabitant of the garden wood-pile.

Agrocybe species
(*top*) one of those with the lovable woolly feet clinging to their chosen piece of wood.

Helvella macropus
(*lower*) unmistakably itself in the curious and remarkable variety of forms, with no two even nearly alike.

137

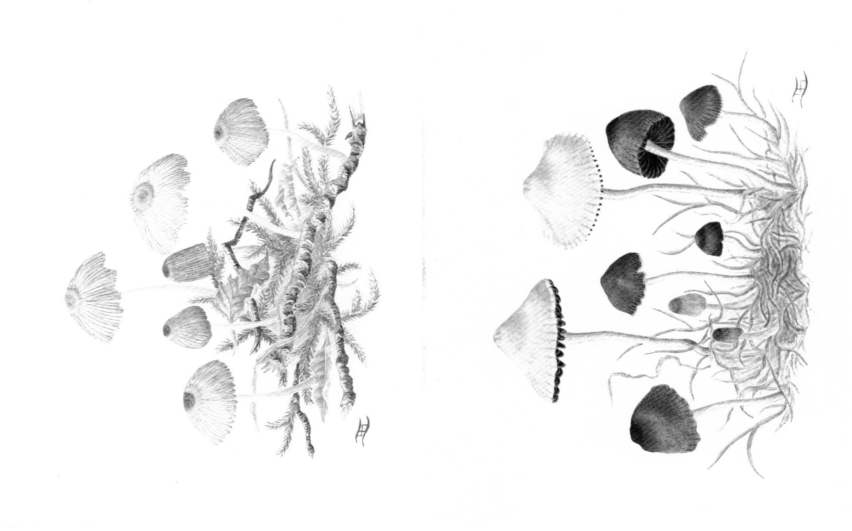
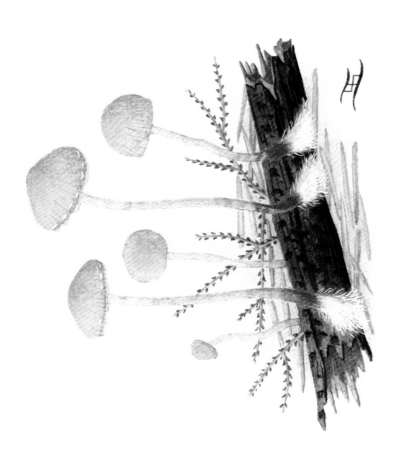
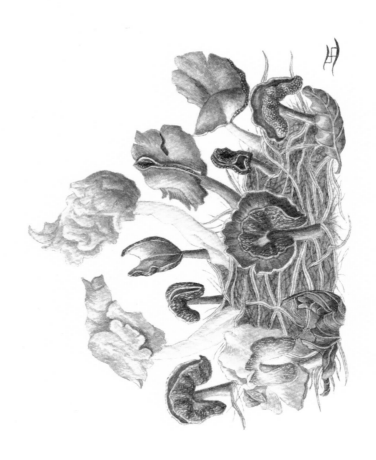

Amanita jonquillea
(*top*) so much in this small being
to please, fawn scales on pale
gold, delicate collarettes on a stalk
later girdled with darker colour
and the strange base cushion from
which it emerges.

Inocybe asterospora
(*lower*) a very decorative variation
on the ever-entrancing Inocybe
theme, with ivory openings where
the caps divide to show the
underlay and gills.

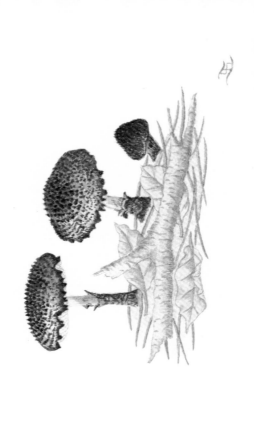

Lepiota negromarginata
appeared beneath lilac and was most endearing, with tiny pyramid scales on its
cap and feet in speckled stockings.

Psathyrella species
(*top*) favoured bare ground under
raspberry canes growing by a
larch fence and was bewitching
with velvet mahogany caps, not to
mention its silken feet.

Laccaria laccata var.
amethystina
(*lower*) speaks for itself with its
delicious colour contrasting most
satisfyingly with the beech leaves.

Index